DARING
&
DISRUPTIVE

Unleashing the Entrepreneur

LISA MESSENGER

NORTH STAR WAY

NEW YORK   LONDON   TORONTO   SYDNEY   NEW DELHI

NORTH
STAR
WAY

North Star Way
An Imprint of Simon & Schuster, Inc.
1230 Avenue of the Americas
New York, NY 10020

First North Star Way trade paperback edition September 2016

NORTH STAR WAY and colophon are trademarks of Simon & Schuster, Inc.

For information about special discounts for bulk purchases,
please contact Simon & Schuster Special Sales at 1-866-506-1949
or business@simonandschuster.com.

The North Star Way Speakers Bureau can bring authors to your live event.
For more information or to book an event contact the North Star Way Speakers
Bureau at 1-212-698-8888 or visit our website at www.thenorthstarway.com.

Manufactured in the United States of America

10 9 8 7 6 5 4 3 2 1

Library of Congress Cataloging-in-Publication Data
Names: Messenger, Lisa, author.
Title: Daring & disruptive : unleashing the entrepreneur / Lisa Messenger.
Other titles: Daring and disruptive
Description: New York : North Star Way, 2016.
Identifiers: LCCN 2016005777| ISBN 9781501135866
(trade paperback) | ISBN 9781501135873 (ebook)
Subjects: LCSH: Entrepreneurship. | Creative ability in business. |
Success in business. | BISAC: BUSINESS & ECONOMICS /
Entrepreneurship. | BUSINESS & ECONOMICS / Motivational. |
BIOGRAPHY & AUTOBIOGRAPHY / Business.
Classification: LCC HB615 .M477 2016 | DDC 658.1/1--dc23

ISBN 978-1-5011-3586-6
ISBN 978-1-5011-3587-3 (ebook)

DARING
&
DISRUPTIVE

here's to the crazy ones. the

the troublemakers the round peg

the ones whe

they're not fond of rules and they

You can quote them, disagree with them

About the only

Because they change thing

They imagine They invent

They c

They push the human

Maybe

How else can you stare at an e

Or sit in silence and hear a s

Or gaze at a red planet and

And while some may see them as

Becaus

think they can change the World

misfits the rebels.

in the square holes.

see things differently.

have no respect for the status quo.

glorify them or vilify them.

thing you can't do is ignore them.

They heal. They explore

reate. They inspire

race forward.

they have to be crazy...

mpty canvas and see a work of art?

ng that's never been written?

see a laboratory on wheels?...

the crazy ones, we see genius.

the people crazy enough to

are the ones that do.   — Steve Jobs / App

CONTENTS

DARING

adjective

to bravely go where others won't.

DISRUPTIVE

adjective

to shake things up and make your mark on the world.

INTRODUCTION

I'm an ideas person. I'm not interested in details; I'm all about the big picture. So in March 2013, when I launched a print magazine into a highly unstable, fractious market where magazines were dropping like flies, I'm pretty sure people thought I had no idea what I was doing.

To the outside world, it may have seemed like a crazy, uncalculated, and unthinkably risky move. But to me, launching the *Collective Hub*™ was just another disruptive play based largely on gut and intuition; something I'd wanted to do for a while and finally felt that the timing, for me, was right.

Even though I didn't have any experience (read: zilch) in the industry, even though no one on my team at the time did either, these were just minor details.

It's the way I love to do life—to disrupt, challenge, inspire, and flip just about anything flippable on its head. I love to be purposefully counterintuitive on almost every level. When you say zig, I say zag, and I wouldn't have it any other way.

I've been running my own businesses for over a decade, and I'm being sincere when I say that even when I hate it, I love it. Business is in my veins and in every part of my DNA. I wasn't one of those lemonade-selling kids on the front lawn (possibly because we lived miles from anywhere, so I spent my days riding my horse and putting on plays for the family), but when the time came to run my own show, my blood was pumping with a desire to play a big game and build a platform of good in the world.

Before I launched the magazine, I was—and still am—a serial entrepreneur. I brokered sponsorship deals for the likes of Barry Humphries, the Wiggles, and Cirque du Soleil; ran a public relations agency; founded a marketing company; and dabbled in property, among other things. I wear the badge of serial entrepreneur proudly.

Then, after publishing my first book in 2004, I redirected my marketing and sponsorship skills to the world of book publishing, with just a hint of experience to draw on: a one-day self-publishing workshop and a one-day publishing workshop—yep, that was it!

But before long, I'd authored a ton of books and my company had published more than four hundred books for others.

As a self-confessed, slightly crazy entrepreneur who spends a good deal of my life in meetings, at events, and increasingly in front of people on the stage or on TV, I am always talking to people—thousands every week in some form or another. I love hearing their stories and sharing mine. And there is one question I am asked over and over again, consisting of five little words: How do you do it?

How do you launch a business in a completely new industry? How do you forge ahead when others are retreating? How do you find a yes when everyone is saying no? How do you keep the faith on the tough days, and plow forward when the shit is hitting the fan? How do you make your entrepreneurial dreams come true?

These pages are my response to that: my brain dump, my thoughts and philosophies on business that hopefully go some way to explaining how, as an entrepreneur proudly pushing the limits, I go about business and this thing we call life.

I'm no expert. But after many years of owning my own businesses—some successful and some fairly spectacular failures—what I can offer is a smorgasbord of my own experiences that I hope will resonate with you and help you navigate your own situation. While I talk about the magazine's journey and the business lessons to draw from it, this book is not the complete magazine tell-all—that will come when we're a little older.

These pages are written through the filter of my heart—less so from my head. They're about passion and desire, making a lasting impression on this world. This book is designed to make you think and to encourage you to dig deep—to stay on target, to back yourself, to remain true to your ideas. Because honestly, no one else will. And when you're $300,000 into an idea and a little unsure just how far or even if it will fly, you'll need to draw on those reserves.

I hope that after reading this, you feel inspired to take risks, disrupt, be passionate, find your purpose, surround yourself with an awesome team, and never give up. I know unwaveringly in every single cell of my body that absolutely anything in this world is possible. Anything. Absolutely anything. Yes, it is.

Getting words onto a page is not usually an issue for me, and when the passion is pumping and the juices flowing, my hands can hardly keep up with my brain. The philosophies shoot out of me at warp speed. Then my team—God love them—took me aside and said the text needed more of "me" in there, with more stories, anecdotes, and the actual stuff that has formed these philosophies over many years.

Well, that was hard—mostly because I take what I need from the past, learn from it, and move on very quickly, living in the present and harnessing the future. Most of what I do now is intuitive, so it's tricky to reverse-engineer my whole way of thinking in order to unpack the processes.

But I knew it would be worth it to go there, because I wanted this book to be soulful, punchy, profound, and poetic. I want every single sentence to evoke emotion in you; I want to elicit heartfelt tears in one paragraph, and in the next, have you so angry and in so much pain that you want to scream from the rooftops and run out and make massive changes in the world.

Personally, I have been through plenty of peaks and troughs, including some very dark periods in my life marred by depression, estrangement from my family, a failed marriage, and a not-so-pretty love affair with alcohol.

As a result, it has been my purposeful, conscious mandate to live a full, deep, rich, soul-satisfying, and successful life for the Lisa who almost didn't make it.

For those who are just like the old me, who are searching for a beacon of hope to spur them on in their quest to make a mark on this world—business or otherwise—and for those riding the wave of life high and wide, relishing the adventure, and soaking up every morsel of helpful advice they can find to be the best version of themselves—to all these people, I say, life is a choice.

I believe we all have a choice to make at every single turn. People tend to overthink things and for a multitude of reasons hold themselves back—be it through fear (of failure or of success), self-sabotage, feelings of inadequacy, or a whole host of other emotions. But we create our own realities and are ultimately responsible for what happens in our lives. Of course bad, unexpected stuff still happens, but it's how we choose to deal with the darker moments that makes all the difference.

And it's the rockier parts of our journey that make us stronger, more self-aware, more passionate, and ultimately, more grateful. So as the words start to roll out of me, this is the backdrop against which I write.

We are not our past. We are not just our stories. But they do shape and define our future and make us the people we are today. When we choose to see the positive in people, good things and great situations start to happen.

Every single one of us has the possibility to be extraordinary and really shake things up. So as you read, I hope something stirs within you to be more renegade, disruptive, and confident; to be a game changer, a thought leader, a rule breaker, and a style maker. After all, is there any other way? Let the business—and life—revolution and movement march on.

What a crazy roller coaster of a ride the start-up life is

Don't

BE PEDESTRIAN,
beige or
follow the
status quo

MAKE
CHANGE

→ HAVE ←
ATTITUDE

_____

Live life
viscerally

Get up when you
FALL DOWN

be
BRAVE
be BOLD
BE Gutsy *
EXPOSE
yourself
to the
BEST
things
that humans
have DONE
& bring them
into your
BUSINESS

BELIEVE

To succeed in business—hell, to succeed in anything in life—you must have an unwavering, insatiable, tenacious belief in yourself. You have to be able to back yourself, to harbor that kind of unbridled passion for winning that will stop at nothing until you reach your goals.

This is crucial. It's more than crucial. It's really the only thing that matters—more than your ideas, more than your products, more than your backers and funders and supporters. Because even with all of those, you will get knocked down thousands of times, over and over. You will have the door slammed in your face and you will hear the word *no* so often, you'd swear you were asking a toddler to get into his car seat every two minutes.

When we interviewed Jennifer Dulski from the petition-hosting website Change.org—she also spent many years at Yahoo and Google in senior roles—she put it quite eloquently: "Some days are sunny and other days are stormy."

To handle rejection—and the nonstop obstacles that are thrust in the path of all unsuspecting entrepreneurs—you need to find a way to equip yourself with the resilience and the tools to move forward. You'll need the day-to-day good stuff, like tenacity and drive, but even that won't count for much if you don't believe deeply in yourself; you must have an almost irrational self-belief that propels you forward, despite any chaos or failure around you.

As the author Marianne Williamson so powerfully puts it in *A Return to Love*: "Our deepest fear is not that we are inadequate. Our deepest fear is that we are powerful beyond measure. . . . We ask ourselves, Who am I to be brilliant, gorgeous, talented, fabulous? Actually, who are you *not* to be? . . . Your playing small does not serve the world. . . . And as we let our own light shine, we unconsciously give other people permission to do the same."

If you want to move fast and be nimble and flexible, you need to learn to rely on yourself first and foremost, instead of waiting around for the approval and external validation of others. It's true, what we entrepreneurs say: If you wait to do anything by focus group, you'll be waiting a ridiculously long time. And for those of us who are instant-gratification junkies, that just doesn't cut it.

Sometimes you just have to back yourself and move forward, taking advice only from people you deeply trust and whose opinions you respect and value. It's about taking personal responsibility for your own growth and never ever giving up on the ideas that you feel genuinely have merit. You simply can't afford to if you want to take any ground or have any kind of serious impact.

When I decided to start a magazine, my marketing director and I began meeting with people. With marketing materials created for something that didn't actually exist (vaporware, I like to call it), we hit the phones and the pavement and we hit them hard. We had just over a hundred meetings with corporate head honchos, top media buyers, some of the nation's most successful entrepreneurs—basically, any key influencers or decision-makers we felt could partner with us to get the project off the ground. Few Australian corporations were left unturned!

We were both certain that we had a killer idea, but it was an epic mission. Even with our absolute and unwavering belief that we had a product the market was ready to support, the metaphoric door slamming, email avoidance, and downright noes started to wear a little thin. But we kept brushing the dust off our well-worn entrepreneurial sleeves, and we kept going.

After stalking the then chief marketing officer of a major Australian bank for at least three months, late one night I sent him a tweet. I had exhausted all the other platforms, and I knew he was a prolific user of social media. Within about four minutes I had a reply: "How about 2 pm tomorrow?"

Then I was momentarily filled with pure terror. In fact I can feel it still; as I write this, the emotion comes flooding straight back. The thing was, we'd had so many noes and I knew in my heart that this bank and their campaign at the time, which was all about empowering people to dream and be the best in life that they could be, was the corporation to get on board. Their messaging was a perfect alignment, and if they said yes, it would open incredible doors. But what if they said no?

It was almost easier to run the other way. I could handle other setbacks, but to get a definitive no from them? That would have been a massive blow. I almost didn't want to have the meeting, because it meant I would have my answer, one way or the other.

In fact, for the briefest moment, I actually considered not

going, canceling the meeting. Madness, I know. But sometimes when you are on that knife's edge of make-or-break, the pain can be almost unbearable, even for the most positive among us.

Of course I sucked it up. I drew on every last bit of resolve and self-belief. With everything I had in me, I forced myself to walk through the doors of the unknown. I put on my best clothes—the ones that made me feel most confident and grounded me in the energy I needed to bring—and I went to the meeting.

I talked with a man I didn't know—the man, the one who could change everything. A man who directed the bank's marketing budget, the top dog. A man who, forty minutes into the conversation, turned to me and asked how much money I needed.

I threw a figure at him—a good one that would be enough to get us seriously moving—and he agreed. He agreed! With three simple words that I will never forget, "We'll do it," the *Collective Hub*™ was officially born.

Inside my head, a full marching band was under way, an entire cheering squad—my brain could hardly contain the excitement and exhilaration of that moment! But I sat completely composed, as if that kind of thing happened for us every day, and then I thanked him and left his office. I put my dark sunglasses on and walked into their elevator—and then I burst into tears.

They began to flow like a river once dammed up whose waters had finally been released; it was a massive outpouring of emotion, relief, gratitude, excitement, and validation.

My marketing director was waiting in the foyer, as we had another meeting lined up straight afterward. I couldn't talk. I just ushered her outside, and once we were there, she gave me a big hug. "Oh, it's okay, we'll be okay," she said kindly. She thought we'd received yet another no, and she knew how crushing this one was.

I turned to her, the tears now in full flood—there may have even been a few wretched, emotional sobs—and choked out, "It's okay; he said yes. He said YES! HE SAID YES!"

He could have said yes to $5,000 or $500,000; the amount was irrelevant. What mattered was that finally my dogged, irrational, tenacious self-belief had paid off. Someone saw the vision and got it. Our idea was validated, not by just any old backer, but by one of the biggest banks in the country.

And now, just as important, I was accountable to someone bigger than me. Sometimes that's all it takes to kick things off at the next level. I had someone who believed in me and the dream I had for the magazine, and I wasn't going to let him down.

To paint a picture of the extent of the self-belief I really needed at that time, I went back to my journals. On a particularly tough day, about two months out from launch, this is what I wrote:

Bring on tears. Permanently going to implode!

IMMENSE PRESSURE 18-hour days. Seven days a week.

cancelled every social engagement. Talking to ~~many~~ lawyers

over office property woes.

stretched on so many ~~levels~~ financially.

TRUSTING MY GUT .

Remembering how much I seriously have my arse on the line her

Don't remember the last time I was so tired. Can see finally

why people have HEART ATTACKS.

cranky and losing it.

Crazy tension. it's total hell! am fighting the battles

that rage ~~aga~~ against my self-belief and self-worth

I know this is the right thing to do, I think this has

merit, I know we can do it, but can't understand how we can be

far behind. FEELS OUT OF CONTROL

keep breathing.

remember the why.

DIG DEEP. Believe.

At around this time, we had just moved into new premises, as our other office was being renovated for eighteen months. The day we moved in, a water pipe burst. We were told we'd have to move out again because they needed to gut the entire building. It was absolutely the last thing I needed; you could say that the challenges were coming from every direction.

We managed to hold them off for six months, but moved offices temporarily before we launched. We had five months in another location, and although the whole experience was incredibly stressful, it ended up being a blessing in disguise, because we didn't have to pay rent during that time.

It was a reminder that while I couldn't control everything that was happening, I could control how I reacted to it. Some people get into business and then expect others to support them and propel them forward, when the plain truth is that you need to do that for yourself. The buck always stops with you. While I suddenly had one of the biggest banks in the country in our corner with the magazine, it was still up to me to make this thing happen. It was still up to me to make the project they had just invested in a success.

When it gets hard, you are still the one left holding on to things—both good and bad. I laugh now, but there have been times when I've seen staff members leave the company to go on to other opportunities and, truth be told, I wanted to walk out with them! *You can leave,* I thought. *I'm stuck here.*

So how do we get self-belief embedded deep into our souls, into the very marrow of our bones? Because saying we need this is one thing, but building belief in ourselves is entirely another matter.

We are surrounded by external noise, people offering well-intended advice and opinions on what to do and when, or how not to be and why. You need to differentiate advice that is smart and relevant enough to take on board from the stuff that you need to let float on by.

I can speak only from my experience and the personal development I've engaged in, but I believe a certain level of self-belief is with you from birth and is fostered or quashed as you grow into an adult.

As your belief in yourself grows over time when you achieve and do well in situations, it's almost as if you subconsciously build a file of intelligence on yourself that proves you're capable and clever, that your gut instinct can be trusted and your ideas will stick. An email from a friend that spurs you on, the feeling when you walk away from a meeting and know you've completely nailed it, the moment you step back and know you handled a staff situation well and have learned from less successful attempts in the past. These are all small moments of validation that get stored in your self-belief bank, ready for you to draw upon when you feel your own supply dwindling.

My very first business was a sponsorship agency. I flung the doors open wide on October 22, 2001, with two secondhand desks (both with broken legs, which I propped up with telephone books) and a PO box at Sydney's prestigious Australia Square, which I picked to sound swanky. I still have the same address all these years later, although I've only physically been there once; that entire time, our mail has been redirected.

I moved a phone from my living room to my "new office"—one door away in the spare bedroom—ordered some business cards, and stocked up on Post-its. Voilà! I was open for business.

Unfortunately, I launched about five weeks after the fateful terrorist attacks of September 11, 2001. It was possibly the worst time to be rolling up my entrepreneurial sleeves. Trying to procure money during such an economic downturn caused my father such heart palpitations that it was the only time I've ever seen my tough, strong, and incredibly confident father cry.

And in hindsight, he was right. I landed some hotshot clients (I had solid experience, but I also had the gift of gab), but corporate dollars were not forthcoming for them, no matter how hard I tried or where I turned for sponsorship. So I ate a lot of cans of spaghetti and baked beans during those first few months.

It would have been flat-out easy to walk away. I was lucky in that I had a few job offers, should I ever have wanted to work for an employer again, but I didn't. Looking back, I don't remember ever entertaining that thought, even when there wasn't enough cash in the bank to pay for the next taxi to the next meeting or the bunch of flowers required to say thank-you to a client.

Sure, I had some blind optimism to thank for the decision to keep forging ahead, knowing success was just around the corner, but the bulk of my behavior centered around a deep, resolute belief that I had the right combination of skills, personality, experience, and ideas to create a valuable market proposition.

So I banged on more doors, scheduled more meetings, made more pitches, and generally worked my behind off until the validation of my own self-belief finally showed up. With every deal I achieved and new client that I signed, my bank of self-belief grew.

An unexpected break came when the editor of *Marketing* magazine offered to publish my thoughts in a letter to the editor, after I sent a rather abrupt retort to him regarding an article from one of his staff that suggested sponsorship could be brokered only in the traditional gold, silver, and bronze way. Never having written much before, but passionately believing in my views, I furiously banged out a thousand words of literary brilliance and well-structured argument—I hope you're picking up on the sarcasm—and hit send.

He published the entire thing, word for word. I had never cried so much with excitement. That article and several big strategic partnerships I eventually landed meant that I could refill the stationery cupboard and return to eating three well-balanced meals a day.

An explosion of self-belief results when we receive validation from others after a hard-fought slog. As I look back over the years, there are hundreds and hundreds of moments that can drop me to my knees in appreciation. Two instantly come to mind.

The first was in my early days of business and was thanks to the surfing all-star Barton Lynch (1988 world pro tour champion, Pipeliner, and all-around legend). While learning to surf—to chase and impress a boy, side point—I became obsessed with the pastime (after my third time in the waves) and went on a shopping frenzy to gather almost everything the world had to offer beginners.

So I had all the gear, but there were no books for people like me. Surely I could fill this market gap? I found Barton's email address and told him all about my idea. Within ten minutes he replied, saying he loved the idea but was currently in Hawaii and would be back in three weeks.

It was just a hint of external validation, but I ran with it like a wild beast. I was head over heels in love with the book idea and believed it had strong market capabilities, and the mere fact that a marketing-savvy world champion surfer also loved the idea and wanted to talk about it validated it. My gut propelled the entire project forward. Within a day, the marketing materials were designed and I'd begun searching for corporate partnerships to fund the project. Eventually, I published a series of books in conjunction with Barton.

The second moment was early in the life of the magazine in October 2013, when I was invited to observe a front-page editorial meeting at the *New York Times*. There was only one other non-newspaper person there, and he just happened to be an advisor to the British prime minister.

Here I was, in one of the most prestigious newsrooms on the entire planet, listening to their strategy and watching closely as they laid out their decision-making process. We're talking the home of the *New York Times* bestseller list, which most authors would virtually sell their left arm to be a part of—the people who released the Pentagon Papers in 1971 and the winner of 117 Pulitzer Prizes, more than any other news organization in the world.

So here I was sitting in a room full of eighteen newspaper heavyweights. I was in total dizzy, dreamy awe. At that point, we had produced only four issues of the magazine.

The Only person who can stop you from achieving is you. Get up when you stumble, try another path when a brick wall appears and forge ahead with resolute self-belief even when the world screams "no!"

Sitting inside that room, watching talking heads around the oval table deliberating and decision-making in action, I realized that while they were talking about different people in different cities doing different things, our editorial meeting back home—with far fewer people in a room an eighth the size of theirs—played out in similar fashion. We talked, asked questions, and argued points just as they did.

What I thought I would take from that meeting was a big fat *wow*, and I did, but in a completely different way than I expected. I was in a situation that I thought was largely unattainable, but it left me with an absolutely unwavering assurance that everyone is equal and that truly anything is possible.

It was the biggest endorsement for this media apprentice, who had no business partners, media mentors, or venture capitalists in my camp, just a bloody big dream.

My very presence in that room told me—just as I knew, and just as I'd been telling brands, media buyers, publicists, and generally anyone who would listen—that this magazine had legs. It had a place in the market and a purpose to fulfill, and we were on the right track. The freakin' *New York Times* saw it, and so did I.

I'll never forget those moments of validation, as they lit the fire under my own self-belief and gave me that extra boost of energy I needed to boldly move forward. It's key to surround yourself with positive, helpful people. People who will propel you forward rather than pull you, or your ideas, back—fabulous sharp-minded people who are creative but also savvy, who are dreamers and thinkers but also doers, and who say yes more than they say no; those who are brave and courageous.

You also need to protect yourself from those who pull you down, who sap you of your energy and positivity, who trample on your ideas or quash your innovation; those who stop you from becoming the very best version of yourself.

And it doesn't matter what age or stage you are at. Many people sabotage their own ideas because they think they are too old or too young to embark on a new dream; that they've left their run for far too late or that they don't have the age, wisdom, or experience to take on something so big.

When it came to the magazine, I could have brushed it aside, saying I was too old to start such a courageous venture that could take years to mature—especially when I had limited experience in that specific field. Or I could have said I'm too young for this. Where are the years of maturity and industry know-how behind me? I need more time to immerse myself in this new world, to talk with the gurus and learn from the best.

Luckily, neither thought crossed my mind. Too old. Too young. What is the "normal age" to achieve things, anyway? Michael Jackson had his first hit single as a solo performer at the age of thirteen. Yet Andrea Bocelli didn't even make his first demo until he was in his mid-thirties, and at seventy-one, Coco Chanel reestablished her couture house after a sixteen-year absence.

Surely the only limiting factor can be giving in to the status quo? As one sage said, "Age is an issue of mind over matter. If you don't mind, it doesn't matter." Or as Muhammad Ali put it, "Age is whatever you think it is."

As you begin to believe in yourself, you will have less and less need for external validation. This is when you'll really start to shine in whatever situations you are presented with. You will also begin to believe in your ability to make good decisions based on your intuition.

I've been known for saying that I run my business on 95 percent gut feel and 5 percent "other," whatever the other might actually be. Try telling that to your CFO. Just after the magazine started, I had to "break up" with him for four months. He just could not understand how on earth I was taking such a massive risk and still surviving. I would sit in meetings with a calm smile on my face and say things like "It's okay—it will be fine," with an innate knowledge that it really would be, that there was a serious market value proposition attached. Unquestionably.

My CFO didn't quite agree. As his face turned redder and redder and he pumped his finger at a bottom line that would indicate anything but okay, we decided to call it quits, have some space, take a break, find ourselves. It didn't faze me. Not one bit. Because in my gut, I knew this thing would fly.

If I had a dollar for every time an entrepreneur has told me that he or she should have used his or her gut and intuition more,

I would be a very rich lady. But they are so right. I believe that as an entrepreneur, you build up a very healthy and high-functioning gut instinct by being an insatiable learner who pulls together every morsel of information from everything you experience. Every deal done or not done, every meeting or event attended, every business idea devised and every business idea put into action, every staff situation encountered (positive and negative), every failure, every tricky client problem solved and every hurdle overcome—all add to your ability to react, to forecast, and to make decisions based on your previous experiences.

We create our own sixth sense, based on our ability to draw on all the pockets of information we have stored inside our brains and hearts to make clever, intuitive decisions at every turn, bringing together both natural and nurtured skills and the tools we have amassed along the way.

Your intuition is so intrinsically a part of who you are that you almost find it hard to deconstruct, unpack, or reverse-engineer it. I didn't just wake up one day and have this built-in sense of it. It came as a result of years and years of personal development, learning, and experience. But I also truly believe that most entre-preneurs know their market intimately. They know the key play-ers and digest as much history and information as they can on an industry (even if they have just gotten into it and are disrupt-ing it). And they do this because they are hungry for knowledge and empowerment, which is a huge advantage when it comes to decision-making.

If I didn't have a strong belief in my intuition and gut instinct, I would possibly collapse. I say this because without this belief, I'd probably focus solely on the imminent challenges of being in business, instead of focusing on the vision, purpose, or potential opportunity in every situation.

Learning to rely on your intuition also comes from learning about yourself—every corner of your psyche—and becoming aware of the good, bad, ugly, and wonderful that makes you, you. Then you work out which situations you can best trust yourself in, and put tools, mechanisms, structures, processes, and teams in place to fill in the gaps and shortfalls. This way, nothing will ever be insurmountable or scary.

Bradley Trevor Greive (BTG), the author of the bestselling *The Blue Day Book* (which has now sold over 25 million copies), is a dear friend of mine with a beautiful spirit and a sharp mind. When we interviewed him for the magazine, he talked about how he was rejected hundreds of times with that manuscript before someone finally gave him a shot.

"There are only three types of ideas: good, bad, and ugly," he told me. "Bad ideas despoil other ideas and should be tossed aside immediately. Ugly ideas should be reexamined in a new light to see if in fact they have some hidden merit, as many do. But really good ideas need to be fought for. *The Blue Day Book* was a good idea—I knew it in my bones. I knew it because there was nothing like it at the time and I knew it because it made me laugh out loud again and again. So I stuck with it.

"And every time I received a dismissive rejection letter, I chose to regard it as tangible proof that I was one step closer to finding the literary agent and publisher I deserved—and in the end, like everyone else who has simply refused to give up, I was proved right."

BTG was once an elite combat soldier in the army, which is vital to know for what he told me next: "I am honestly in awe of successful creative professionals and entrepreneurs who do not have the brutal military background that I have. I would be nowhere without the training I received as a young paratrooper commander. Even when things go wrong, I enjoy the harsh comfort of always knowing I've been through worse. Ultimately, when our mortal flesh fails us, as it invariably must, it all comes down to sheer will. I have seen hard men break and others thrive in the exact same circumstances—the difference was their sense of purpose and self-belief, and the ability to laugh at themselves."

As an entrepreneur, you forge ahead against the odds and you're told no endless times, but remember that the material life around us was created by people no smarter than you. You are no less capable of changing the world than the next person.

You have just as many hours in the day as Steve Jobs did or as Oprah Winfrey or Richard Branson does.

This incredible thought from the writer C. JoyBell C. ripped straight to my core the first time I heard it, and it still rings just as deep whenever I hear it now: "The only person who can pull me down is myself, and I'm not going to let myself pull me down anymore."

We are limited only by our own belief systems, our own ways that we perpetuate self-sabotage. You need to have the confidence and self-belief that if you get thrown to the wolves (and you will be), you'll have the strength to come out leading the pack.

BACK your IDEAS

PLAY the GAME of life FEROCIOUSLY

BELIEVE in yourself

overcome OBSTACLES

surround
yourself
with those who
BUILD
you up

DREAM BIG!*
never stop
believing

FEAR.LESS.

Fear is technically, by definition, an "unpleasant emotion caused by the threat of danger, pain, or harm." Wait up—are you kidding? Not that I planned to take on the world of dictionaries here, but describing fear as "unpleasant"? I don't think so. Horrific, gut-wrenching, sickening, crippling—these are more appropriate words to describe fear. But unpleasant? Please. Unpleasant doesn't even begin to cover it.

Fear in business is commonplace. There's fear of failure and, often even bigger, fear of success. There's also the fear of rapid growth (or not enough growth), worries that we won't have the cash to pay the bills, that our competitors will run faster or quash us, that our suppliers will fall through or our products will turn up faulty, that deals will sour, that clients will be unhappy, that someone will sue us, or that we won't get the revenue needed this month to pay our staff.

The brain is a truly powerful thing, and if we let it, we can think and project fear until it paralyzes us. But if that's the case, then surely we can think and project the opposite.

I have always loved this quote from the famed psychiatrist Karl Menninger, who says: "Fears are educated into us, and can, if we wish, be educated out." Another I refer to often is from the amazing Brené Brown, whom we have featured in the *Collective Hub*™

and who once told Oprah, "We're all afraid. We just have to get to the point where we understand it doesn't mean we can't also be brave."

Without realizing it, I have become less and less fearful in business. It wasn't really until I started getting asked (daily) how I overcame my fear and why I was so fearless that I recognized the shift. Nothing really frightens me in a business sense, or, for that matter, personally.

As I started trying to unpack my thoughts for the pages of this book, I realized how hard it is to reverse-engineer what got you to a certain place. I started to really look at my own behaviors, to try to make some logical sense of the seemingly nonlogical decisions I've made or the difficult scenarios I've overcome.

Here's what I realized upfront. I'm obviously not an expert on the science of the brain, but I am qualified to share my own experiences. So while the process may take some time, I believe it is not impossible to retrain a fear-prone brain, because while fear is real, it is largely perceived.

The entrepreneur who can handle fear (which in my mind is a perceived threat)—with a healthy respect for any danger (which constitutes a real threat) in any given situation—will end up with the competitive edge.

I really hope no one takes me up on this, but it has crossed my mind that if I believe in myself and this theory so much, then perhaps I need to put my money where my mouth is. I have an irrational fear of cockroaches. I can't stand being anywhere near them. But I know that they pose no actual danger to me.

I think I am almost ready to put myself to this test by immersing myself in a glass container full of the filthy little critters. I do the equivalent in business, day in and day out, and it has become such a natural and inherent part of my DNA that I think I want to test it out beyond the realms of business. Craziness, I know.

I was once petrified of public speaking; I hated it more than the thought of death. Today I'm an over-sharer who will rant and rave at length with even the whiff of a public platform in the offing, but that wasn't always the case. Wind back the clock a decade or so, and I was a very different Lisa.

Whenever I was asked to speak, I would be sick for days beforehand. My stomach would be in knots to the point that I'd hardly eat and I'd become increasingly frustrating to those around me, who had to endure the brunt of my pain. Finally, sweaty, with my hands shaking (unglamorously) and my mouth dry, I'd go onstage and stumble through whatever I had to say from printed notes, usually as I stood behind (and clung desperately to) a lectern.

It was hideous and so was I, unfortunately. Just like Richard Branson, who had to train himself to become a public speaker by practicing the craft and changing the way he let himself think about it.

My fear of public speaking is one of the reasons I published my first book *Happiness Is . . .* (a coffee table book about what makes Australians happy), because I subconsciously knew that by doing so, I would be forced to speak in public as part of the promotional schedule. It may sound nuts—that I would knowingly force myself into a situation I despised—but perhaps I was channeling a little

Eleanor Roosevelt: "You gain strength, courage and confidence by every experience in which you really stop to look fear in the face. You must do the thing which you think you cannot do."

On the night of the book's launch, in front of a room of politicians, authors, musicians, and publicists, I downed a glass of champagne or two (I was still drinking at this point) and then stood up and read my speech. I *read* it. When I look at the video of that day, I was stamping my feet, shifting from one foot to the other, grabbing the side of my dress, refusing to look at the audience or make eye contact of any sort, shaking—in other words, was essentially terrified.

The audience was silent—I think they saw my pain. They clapped, of course, but it was probably more out of relief than anything else. Despite the poor start, I kept going with the plan.

As part of the publicity schedule, I collaborated with a well-known women's network to speak at three breakfasts across the country; I was to talk about happiness, the book's journey from idea to reality, and my thoughts on entrepreneurialism and women in business. At each venue, eight hundred women would be staring back at me and hanging on my every word.

So I printed out my notes and away I went to the first of the three breakfasts in Sydney, reading the speech verbatim yet again. I never made it to Melbourne or Brisbane. Not because I pulled out, but because they did. The breakfasts went ahead as planned but without the main talent (or lack of) . . . me. Clearly I was so nauseatingly bad that I wasn't even invited back to my own breakfast.

About a year later, I was asked to speak alongside a prominent

Australian entrepreneur who was also a whiz at public speaking. It was a big gig, and I'm not sure how I landed a spot beside him or why I agreed to it—I must have been going back into the "you must overcome this" ring for another round.

Onstage, I stood there and looked at the screen behind me the entire time, apart from a few quick glances from the stage floor to the audience, back to the stage floor, before settling on the screen again. In the quick peeps I managed to send the audience's way, I remember vividly that they were deadpan. I had to speak for an hour but had about ten minutes worth of material. I walked off the stage horrified with myself. Horrible. Even my diplomatic, hugely encouraging, glass-is-definitely-half-full sidekick (who is now my deputy editor), who could always find something positive to say about everything, was stuck for words.

I didn't go back onto a stage for three years. That moment threw me, deeply. It also annoyed me because I knew that one of the best and quickest ways to reach people is to get in front of groups of them. Face-to-face meetings are great when called for, but there are only so many people you can reach with the time that you have, and meetings offer very little leverage. I wanted to speak to hundreds and thousands of people, but I was paralyzed.

Then one day one of my staff sneakily booked an event into my agenda. I wasn't happy about it, but we agreed it was necessary. Cue guts of steel because that's what it took to get me back up onstage. It was a half-hour keynote with a prominent magazine editor and some health industry heavyweights, and the topic was, ironically, confidence.

You can't bottle fear, but it doesn't have to drown you.

I was practicing in the corridor beforehand and felt utterly un-qualified for the task ahead of me, but no one would have known it, because I threw myself up there like a new person. It was far from awesome, but it was well clear of dreadful, too. The time away must have helped with my confidence, because in contrast to my previous speaking engagements, I left that event feeling as if I hadn't totally messed it up.

One speaking opportunity then began rolling into another. Slowly, although I was still full of nerves at the start of each gig, I started to find my mojo. I've always said that you can't make a difference by being a shrinking violet, and now it was time to start walking the walk.

So what actually happened that gave me the confidence to en-gage? In that lengthy period of soul-searching and time away from public speaking, I realized that I was afraid of being me—and that by trying to do it like so many of my motivational-speaker friends had suggested (write something, memorize it, and regurgitate it), I was tripping myself up.

I have many friends who speak for a living; they deliver highly constructed, compelling, well-crafted presentations. But when I do that, I almost disappear from my own body and I'm thrown into chaos. I'm so busy concentrating on getting the next word memorized that I get lost and lose my connection with myself and with the audience. I become inauthentic and am most definitely not present.

The solution for me was simple: Don't stick to a script. Sud-denly the fear fell away and I could see this actually working.

Those who know me would agree that I'm a little wild, fluid, and impromptu. I can't help but join in when others speak freely and honestly, and I thrive on being just that little bit naughty. So when I'm onstage, there might be a little too much information from time to time and a little craziness mixed with the insight and lessons, but at least I'm up there, smashing my fear in the face and being true to my own values.

It's the way I can truly be in the moment and present so that my authenticity can shine. And now? I can genuinely say I love public speaking. Because it's no longer about me; it's about what I can share and how I can help others.

For the public speaking pros out there, this may mean little, but for you who aren't—after all, the most common fears in the world are of spiders, snakes, heights, and public speaking—you'll understand how crippling it can be. But whether it's fear of public speaking or fear felt in the routine activities of business, I now try to keep my response to it amazingly simple.

I have taught my brain to race straight to the worst-case scenario. In my mind's eye, I stare at it right in the face and think about how bad it could possibly be. Then I race back from there to the present moment, reverse-engineering the scenarios and evaluating the steps I could take at each juncture to avoid getting to that point. It's almost like a movie clip in high-speed reverse motion, a personal reconnaissance mission so I can spot the dangers and hypothesize about what I would have changed along the way.

And then it's done: I have dealt with the steps in my mind's eye in the most logical way and realized that the worst-case scenario can be dealt with if it in fact comes to pass, taking note of the actions I should take along the way to ensure it doesn't.

While I've had my fair share of sleepless nights in business—usually around anything legal or financial, which when left unattended can overshadow everything else that's going on and sap me of my creative energy—I have found that following this simple method ensures that what needs to be taken care of is tended to. Depending on the size of the problem at hand, this process can happen in as little as a minute, and I've found that it is one of the best ways to overcome fear.

Obviously, other situations will require more time to evaluate all of the steps thoroughly. And in the beginning, the process takes much longer—minutes turn to hours and office thoughts result in sleepless nights. But over time, it can be honed to a few minutes of well-trained brain gymnastics.

I did a quick calculation and realized that if I felt fear three times a day in all my time as an entrepreneur—that seems realistic—I would have practiced this scenario 14,235 times, so it's no wonder I have now whittled the process down to one or two minutes.

As a result, I can honestly say that there's very little I actually fear these days, and when I do, it is more often than not a matter of my letting my brain run away with itself. Don't get me wrong: The danger presented if you are standing on a cliff and thinking about jumping off is very real, but if you deal with your fears as they arise instead of letting them pile up, you will hopefully never reach that point.

A few issues into the magazine's life, I found myself massively beating myself up over our lack of finances. I indulged in a sleepless night of worry. (Why do things always seem so much worse when you are alone in the darkness? I can make something feel at least five times worse when it's really late at night!) As the fear crept in on this lonely Saturday night, I examined the worst-case scenario as per my script (which to be honest *was* pretty bad), and I fought my way back with the list of options before propelling myself into action.

By six the next morning, I had sent a comprehensive email to my management team outlining other potential revenue streams and actionable items. I'd sent emails to my CFO, accountant, and bookkeeper outlining specific reports I wanted on Monday morning. I'd sent an email to my mortgage broker about what liquidating my properties would involve if it should be necessary (I told you, I went to worst-case scenario!). After running my businesses from day one without a cent of borrowed cash, I even thought—very, very briefly—about what the situation would look like if we brought a venture capital partner on board.

As a result, I was able to wake up and enjoy my Sunday again—which so happened to be a gorgeous day in the country in the sunshine with my partner and dog, Benny—because I had faced the fear, picked it apart, and quickly pulled in a team to help me create a multipronged attack to beat the problem.

Fear is often crippling because we hold it in, meaning that we're the only ones to understand it. In writing those emails I was sharing the load with a trusted inner circle who had my back and who would now mull over the current situation with me. That allowed me to refocus my energy to where it was best justified.

I went from beating myself up—never a good place to be—and being annoyed because, despite so much external success, money was suddenly tough and tight again, to acknowledging the extraordinary journey we had made in a short period of time and realizing that we'd just hit a new point of pain that would propel us forward.

We'd made a splash: We'd gone up against the big guns of magazine publishing and were still standing. Remind yourself of how far you've come when you're working your way through turmoil. I had to remember that at the magazine's inception, I'd had only three staff members, and eight months on, that number was fifteen full-timers as well as sixty or so freelancers working for us all over the globe. We were distributed in eleven countries, and within eight more months, we were in more than twenty-two (now it's thirty-seven).

And crucially, we had different revenue streams to buffer the idea as it launched to market, which we've since eliminated while new ones were being created. We did all of this without the help of equity partners or venture capital, so it was no wonder we were feeling the pain.

It takes discipline and a trained brain not to let fear overwhelm you. After my sleepless night, I could have continued to worry about it all weekend and into the next week, or even for weeks, but what would that have achieved? Nothing—although it would have made me sad and frustrated, my team members uninspired and concerned, while the problem remained unsolved.

Instead, I went from briefly feeling like a loser who was scared, worried about the unknown, and not sleeping to feeling supported, informed, and proud. The latter state is certainly a much better place to operate from. And things are often not as bad as they seem under the cloak of darkness.

When I was brand-new in business, I worried if someone had not paid a $200 invoice. But now of course I wouldn't flinch (not because I'm complacent, but because I have systems and processes in place to deal with it). It's incredible that as your business grows in size and age, you can actually become calmer, because you have faced versions of the same scenarios over and over again, meaning that you have also experienced the outcome over and over again in some form. That means you have a set of cards in your head as to all the possible and variable outcomes and can quickly sort through the pack to come up with the variables in any situation.

As they say, you can't sweat the small stuff. When I'm in danger of going down this path, I like to ask myself these questions: Will it matter ten minutes from now? Will it matter ten months from now? Will it matter ten years from now? And if you really want some perspective, will it matter ten decades from now?

Another fear-related approach is to put my head down and avoid looking up. I'm not saying to put your head in the sand and pretend chaos or trouble is not happening all around you. What I mean is that if you decide to do something, then you should just go ahead and do it instead of being paralyzed by the what-ifs your course of action may present. Let your instincts be your guide and refuse to overthink the situation, because overthinking is like cancer to an idea and one of the biggest fear-enablers you will find.

Finally, part of eliminating fear from your life means getting rid of the risk in the first place. While I love to be a risk-taker, the risks I take must be calculated. In my early book publishing days, I was crap at this. We'd charge clients in advance for the books we would produce and progressively pay our production costs on those units as suppliers billed us. Because book production can happen offshore and often involves long periods of time, that meant we were charging for work upwards of two or three months before we were charged the majority of production costs. It meant I was playing a dangerous game.

Fortunately, I devised a strategy to get around it. I learned about the value of trust accounts and began depositing calculated amounts of money, and I was disciplined enough to start putting money aside so we wouldn't be exposed. By doing so, I removed a large amount of fear.

When it comes to finances, if you're not efficient and effective at managing them, then you need to put a team in place to help, or your finances can quickly cripple or paralyze you. Actually, whatever your weak spot is—finances, tax, HR, strategy—make sure you ask for help to plug the gaps. The aim here is to hire your weaknesses. This is essential to letting go of fear.

But when the money pressures arise (and that is ongoing for every stage of business), you might find it hard to rise above them, and as a result, your creativity, vision, and leadership—so essential for entrepreneurs—can suffer. In a start-up, people tend to keep things too close to their chests, fretting that they can't afford to outsource anything or pay for the team they really want and need. This can be a lonely and overwhelming situation to be in. If you have enough passion and you feel like you are on task, don't be afraid to ask for help; you don't want to face every situation alone.

Understanding fear and finding your own way to deal with it allow you to realize that nothing is insurmountable and everything can be overcome. Few things will stand in your way and nothing is impossible when you truly believe that.

I recall featuring the astronaut Chris Hadfield, the first Canadian to walk in space, in the pages of our magazine; few people know real fear quite like he does. The decisions he made during his three trips into space were literally life and death, and during a space walk, he temporarily lost his vision. Just think that through—you're walking in space and you go blind. During the interview, he commented, "It's not just something recreational or theoretical—our mistakes are life or death, and the risks on board are life and death. You have that underpinning of seriousness all the time, so the meetings [on board] have a real purpose." He also talked about how as an astronaut he has had to train his brain not only to deal with fear but to expect it.

When I feel myself succumbing to the fear factor, I often think of Chris. If he could feel the fear and do it anyway, knowing that the worst-case scenario could literally be his swan song—well, surely I can weather any storm my businesses throw at me.

As an entrepreneur, you will be bombarded with fear every week and at every stage of your business life. You will not be immune to it as your business grows, and the potential for disaster will most likely loom even larger. But while you will never eliminate fear and risk completely, you will get better at managing and overcoming it. You cannot bottle it up. You must remember that it is almost always bigger in your head than it is in reality, and that you must retrain your brain to be truly fearless.

DON'T BE AFRAID

or held back by fear it's never as bad as it seems

SHIFT
your
ENERGY

FACE your FEARS

BE the BEST
version
of you

KNOW
YOUR
"WHY"

I'd say my goal in life is pretty simple: I want to live every day as fully as possible, making every second count while I strive to become the very best version of myself I can be. Easy, right?

Well, I try. Whatever comes, let it come. Whatever stays, let it stay. Whatever goes, let it go. These are the words I try to live by—at times, more successfully than others.

I made a very conscious decision in 2004 to turn my life around, and despite the odd unavoidable bump in the road, I haven't let that promise down. When people say, "You're always so happy," or "Gosh, you do a lot," I'm reminded that the lifestyle I lead is purposefully big. It's not an accident; this is the life I chose.

I run at 100 miles an hour in business because I just don't want to waste the opportunities before me. As a result, I set goals and run wildly toward them, much to the amusement and sometimes frustration of those around me.

A lot of motivations spur this, including a desire to make a vast difference in the lives of other people and to demonstrate by my actions and the way I live my life that anything is possible. I have a naturally determined spirit, a disruptive force ingrained deep within that just wants to try something new or prove to others that there's another way.

However, I deeply believe that there is something else that

leads us toward living a full, rich, and successful life—and that is having purpose. Having a "why." As the former U.S. president John F. Kennedy once said: "Efforts and courage are not enough without purpose and direction."

If you're an accomplished entrepreneur, you can readily pick up your skills and your team and traverse multiple industries with varying success, learning the intricacies of that business as you move. And there is absolutely nothing wrong with that. I've done it on multiple occasions, with book publishing and magazines, for example.

But I have never done it just for the sake of money. Financial success is a nice by-product and it absolutely buys freedom and choice, which in turn provides a greater platform for good. But in and of itself, money is not my driver—not even close.

The one time in my life when I threw money at something for money's sake (a respected colleague had a new entrepreneurial venture and I agreed to back it), the whole experience was quite soulless and only reinforced my thinking that as entrepreneurs, we do what we do for many reasons other than the hefty bank balance we (hope to) accumulate.

As a side point, I have a healthy relationship with money and think money is important. For years, this wasn't the case; one of the things that held me back was that I thought money was a dirty word. As a result, I prevented myself from making any significant money and sabotaged my dreams along the way.

When I learned that without money, I have a limited ability to have a platform in the world or to make widespread positive change, my belief system around it changed. I realized that having money and being a good person did not have to be mutually exclusive.

But back to purpose and your sense of why. Many people talk to me about purpose and ask, "Have you found yours?" And then, "If so, how did you find it?" Finding your purpose, your why for your business life—or for your life generally, if you feel as I do that the two are intertwined—is a different journey for everyone. I can speak only from my own experience.

THE JOURNEY OF DISCOVERY

There have been two times in my life when I've felt 100 percent on track or on purpose, and I'm grateful for them both. The first time was when I wrote my first book, *Happiness Is . . .* The second was when I started the *Collective Hub*™. At both times I was incredibly hungry for something new, I was pushed to my limits in the current work I was undertaking, and I was at times angry, frustrated, or generally pissed off at life or work! Who knew that in those moments, you could experience such clarity?

I look back and see these as weighty moments, because to feel pushed so deeply to act by someone or something evokes a hunger and energy like nothing else. And as I look at both moments, I realize once again that you cannot underestimate the power of adversity or the catalysts that occur in your life.

We must get better at recognizing these moments and latching on to the opportunities around them, as these moments of incurable hunger or painful desperation are when the greatest genius appears. In these moments my go-to default mechanism is now "Something wonderful is about to happen." It's a much healthier place from which to reframe a crappy situation.

Happiness Is . . . was ironically born from a place of my being unbelievably unhappy. Seriously! While my work life rolled along, appearing just fine to onlookers, personally I was struggling. For years I really had no notion of who I was; I was living my life according to other people's expectations. I felt like I was treading water: I was in an unhappy marriage, I barely saw my family, whom I'd subconsciously alienated, and I was drinking far too much. What a happy trifecta.

On the outside, things may have appeared okay—pretty rosy, even—but on the inside, I was dying. Truth be told, I hardly recognized myself. The person I knew I was at my core, the determined little world-changer with big ideas, had somehow vanished. Living in perpetual fear, guilt, and remorse is hell.

I knew I had to turn things around, as rock bottom is a pretty horrific and uncomfortable place to be. I was flat-out miserable and longed to escape the situation before it quite possibly gobbled me up. I thought, *I'm going to go on a quest to find what makes people happy.*

So many people want to write a book, but in that moment of absolute desperation, I was fueled to actually go and do it. Without any publishing knowledge whatsoever, I decided to go around Australia on my own search for happiness, to ask people what happiness meant to them. I was on a mission—I knew exactly what I had to do and went about finding a way to do it.

Within weeks, perhaps even days, the change in my outlook was remarkable. You'd hardly recognize me from the shell of a woman I had been before that purposeful moment. I had found my why. It filled me with such a sense of purpose and engagement that suddenly I couldn't wait to jump out of bed each morning and see what the new day would bring.

And along the way, a funny thing happened. Because I was so passionate about the project, motivated by my desire to find happiness, people were drawn to me and my book like a magnet. The serendipity and synchronicity became infectious; so much so that the book went on to sell through the roof. (I sold 36,000 copies, when a bestseller in Australia at the time was just 5,000.)

It was the start of my journey of self-discovery, my finding out who I was and what I wanted out of life, which I ultimately realized included being in business and having a platform to make a positive change in the world.

This was October 2004. I was at rock bottom and seriously craving change, but what I actually found was the drive to transform myself and my direction in life, along with the courage to do the hard work to make it last. My spouse and I ended the marriage and I gave up drinking shortly after. Then I immersed myself in personal development—therapy, courses, meditating; you name it, I did it.

That's not to say I "fixed" myself. Personal development, in my view anyway, is always a work in progress. I approach spiritual development the same way I approach sports. I do a lot to stay active: I dip in and out of surfing, golf, netball, rock climbing, dance, yoga, and boxing, but I'm not obsessed with these activities.

However, I am totally open to going along with absolutely anything with an open mind and a fresh spirit. I believe 100 percent that what we learn is often very similar across all platforms; the teaching methodologies are the main things that differ. I absolutely love going along with anything new, however zany, and if invited, I will always say yes.

This keeps me fresh, invigorated, excited. Doesn't give me opportunity to become complacent or desensitized to new ways of learning. So if someone says, "Come to church with me," I'll go. If someone says, "Come and try this meditation," I'm there. I'm open. I love to explore and dip into and out of all sorts of things that my friends or the people I meet suggest.

THE TURNING POINT

Of everything I did, I made the most significant progress when I enrolled in two highly intensive and cathartic eight-day retreats. These were so full-on, each was said to be the equivalent of attending a weekly therapy session for five years.

I've been to a raw food vegan commune (an experience I won't forget in a hurry—you've never truly stripped back to basics until you've experienced frighteningly communal showers), I've trekked across parts of western India, I've danced to the beat of bongos in both Byron Bay, Australia, and regional Morocco, and I've crawled through sweat lodges in Costa Rica. I'm happy to push myself to the edge in every situation, to live and explore life and suck up every bit that's on offer. But these days, I'm a little gentler on myself when it comes to thrashing out every part of my past in the name of personal development. The hard work has been done and I'm free to live in the now.

Of course, this was my journey for helping me work through my particular issues. It is not a cure-all and the things I did won't work for everyone else, as we all have our own things to deal with as we forge our own path.

I've summarized this painful yet illuminating period of my life into a handful of paragraphs to shine a little light on my own experiences, which almost makes it seem like breaking free from a suffocating marriage and starting my life over were simple processes. They weren't. Those were the toughest few years of my life. But they were also very necessary. I was so miserable and desperate; anything seemed like a great alternative to where I was.

And fortuitously, this period and *Happiness Is . . .* set my business life on a new trajectory. I felt 100 percent on purpose.

IT TAKES HARD WORK

People ask me, "How have you gotten to where you are?" but sometimes, I don't think they're prepared for an honest answer. When I look them straight in the eye and quip, "Ten years of therapy," their response is often silence. Or perhaps a little awkward laughter. Most people are not quite sure what to do with that.

People hear what they want to hear, so I let them make up their own mind. But one thing I know for sure is that there's no such thing as a quick fix. There is no "one size fits all." There is no pill. No guru on a rock to save you (they may offer you advice, but they can't save you). Because you have to do the work. You yourself. Your way. It's your journey. Mine was mine and I figured out what worked for me. But it's not the same for you. Only you can work that out for yourself.

Happiness Is . . .—as well as the business and consumer media around it (thank you, media—I am eternally grateful)—is the reason I was flooded with requests from others to help them publish their books. And seeing a huge gap in the custom-publishing market, I decided to throw myself into an antiquated industry and see if I could shake it up. That would never have happened without the *Happiness Is . . .* journey.

Book publishing became my main business for the next eight years, helping others self-publish in a high-quality way so that their books could hold their own next to books produced by a publishing house, and so that the author also walked away with most of the profits. While traditional publishing definitely has its place, ours was the best model for some.

The business hummed along perfectly fine with a mix of corporate and private clients. We rode out the financial crisis and we were pretty comfortable. But being comfortable is not a good place to be: Are we really doing our best work and being the very best version of ourselves when we're comfortable? Some would say, "Yes, comfortable is enough."

In my view? It's not. Far from it. And so it was once again time to push myself to another level and get comfortable being uncomfortable.

I knew I had a lot more to give, and after almost a decade of publishing books, I was now capable, equipped, solid, and strong enough in my own skin to take on something new. But this time around, when I felt that calling toward the unknown? This time I was armed.

To begin with, I'd overcome big stuff and I also had several successful and some not-so-successful businesses to my name.

But just as important, I'd pushed myself to my limits in my personal life, too. I'd trekked, gone on retreats, traveled, and gathered a whole lot of life experiences in that time.

All of which meant that when my second moment of purpose descended, I came at it with a different kind of desperation—one that was no longer about me.

THE MOMENT OF TRUTH

This time for me, finding my new purpose was very much about allowing myself to drop to a whole new level, to surrender to the universe and almost remove myself from the equation. With every cell in my being, I knew that I had the strength to hand myself over completely and say, "I'm ready for whatever is next, whatever form or incarnation that takes."

It was no longer about fixing me; it was about making a positive impact on the world and leveraging myself forward for the greatest cause possible. I knew there was something more for me, I just needed to work out what it was—and I knew that if I wanted something badly enough and if my intentions were pure enough, it would come.

I'm a spiritual person, so for about four years, I prayed. And I mean prayed to God or the universe (however you feel about the subject). Day in and day out, in every waking moment—and quite possibly in my sleep if you think that's possible.

Yet somehow I was genuinely and completely unattached to the outcome. I just wanted to make my mark on this earth in the way that I was meant to. The mantra I kept repeating was "What is my purpose?" I was ready.

Words will never do it justice to express how deep and ready my call was. I literally said to the universe: "If the best use of me is cleaning toilets in India for the rest of my life, then I will do it." It was the greatest moment of letting go and surrendering I have ever experienced in my entire life. I figuratively surrendered every single cell in my body to whatever the universe had in store. I just knew I was ready for the next step.

And then one day the idea dropped into my heart, into my head, or into my lap (whichever way you think it rolls): I needed to build a community of like-minded people who were clever, informed, creative, and world-changing. It would start with a magazine . . . and so we did it!

To find purpose, I believe you need to bring your entire self to the table: who you are at work, who you are at home, and who you are when you're with your friends or family. In the past, at times I might have kept them all separate and might have been a different Lisa, depending on the situation.

Today I'm the same all around—the over-sharer at the dinner table and from the stage, the visionary around the office table and when planning holidays, the caring friend who also cares about my staff. I know who I am and don't have to keep shifting my energy to suit a new environment. Instead, I can focus all of my energy on engaging with the world and having a positive impact on it.

You also need to let go of other people's expectations and live the life you want and feel you are meant to live. I read a powerful article recently about a palliative care nurse who said that the number one thing people told her on their deathbed was that they wished they had lived their life without the influence or constraint of other people's expectations.

MY MANTRAS

When I looked back at my personal journal entries over the years, these were some of the mantras I repeated to myself throughout my journey:

KNOW YOURSELF. UNDERSTAND YOUR WEAKNESSES, STRENGTHS, BELIEFS, AND VALUES.

• • •

MAKE DISCOVERING YOUR PURPOSE, YOUR PURPOSE. IMAGINE THE IMPOSSIBLE. THAT IS ENOUGH.

• • •

STAY OPEN TO OPPORTUNITIES AND THEN EXPERIMENT, EXPERIMENT, EXPERIMENT. DON'T BE AFRAID OF FAILING.

• • •

BELIEVE YOU ARE GOOD ENOUGH AND THAT NO ONE, AND I MEAN NO ONE, IS BETTER THAN YOU. YOU ARE NOT YOUR PAST AND YOU CAN CREATE ANY FUTURE YOU WANT. WRITE DOWN A LIST OF PEOPLE YOU ADMIRE AND WHY. ADOPT THESE TRAITS AS A WAY FOR YOU TO SHOW UP IN THE WORLD.

• • •

FIND A FORMAT YOU LIKE FOR PERSONAL GROWTH. IT MIGHT BE TO EDUCATE YOURSELF, TRAIN YOURSELF, TALK TO OTHERS, NETWORK, OR FIND A GREAT MENTOR.

• • •

BE A TRAILBLAZER: BREAK THE RULES, DISRUPT, TAKE A DIFFERENT ROAD, AND DO IT FEARLESSLY.

• • •

DEVELOP A THICK SKIN, STRENGTH, AND MATCH FITNESS FOR THE GAME OF LIFE. IT'S IMPERATIVE SO YOU BECOME GRATEFUL FOR REJECTION AND SEE IT AS EXPERIENCE INSTEAD OF A PARALYZER.

• • •

KNOW THAT AT ANY MOMENT IN TIME, YOU CAN CHANGE YOUR ATTITUDE. NO MATTER YOUR PAST FAILURES OR TRIUMPHS, YOU CAN HAVE A POSITIVE MIND-SET ANY TIME YOU CHOOSE.

• • •

DO WHAT YOU LOVE.

• • •

DEVELOP A SPECTACULARLY DIFFERENT APPROACH TO EVERYTHING.

• • •

SET ASIDE TIME TO REFLECT, CHECK IN, AND RECHARGE. FATIGUE CAN MAKE COWARDS OF US ALL.

• • •

NOTICE HOW YOU FEEL. IF YOU ARE ON PURPOSE, YOU WILL FEEL EXCITED, EXHILARATED, FULL OF ADRENALINE, AND ALIVE—THE VERY BEST VERSION OF YOURSELF.

• • •

FEEL THE FEAR AND DO IT ANYWAY.

• • •

ALWAYS BE YOURSELF. STAY GROUNDED AND REMEMBER WHERE YOU CAME FROM.

• • •

JUST START.

• • •

If you're struggling to tune into your purpose, you should listen for consistent statements from people around you. You may be really great at something that you consider just a hobby, but if people keep commenting on how great you are at it, perhaps there's a way to monetize it and take it to your business world. People often see things in us that we haven't recognized in ourselves.

What are the things you do naturally without even thinking about it? Seek creative outlets; try different hobbies and put yourself out there. Live life. Really live it! Paint, draw, doodle, read, sing, knit, do crafts, build, act, cook, photograph, dive, climb, go WILD. Just start doing something. Anything.

KNOW YOUR VALUES

When it comes to purpose, consider your values, as things can quickly deteriorate if you don't. I have found this to be true countless times on my business journey, and if I could get a do-over in some situations, I would have reacted differently. But often knowledge comes in hindsight, and without these misadventures, the learnings would not have come.

Fortunately, all of the decisions I made that didn't sit right were quite small situations and didn't have a huge impact on my business or me.

Before the magazine launched, I approached one of the biggest and most respected people in the global entrepreneurial world. I sent him an email explaining the magazine concept. The next minute, he was on the other end of the phone. He had rung me from his base in the United States. I could hardly believe it! Surely this was unheard of—the bigger people get, the more unreachable they usually become.

I explained that I wanted to interview him to profile him and feature his winning philosophies in the magazine. I was totally flexible. His answer was basically that he was keen to be involved, but that we could access his blog material online and repurpose it how we wanted. I was firm on the fact that we would never repurpose or syndicate content—that every article had to have a fresh component to it, even if it was minimal. That didn't go down so well.

He dug his heels in, even more certain that if the message was good, he had already written it. I disagreed and hoped that I could draw a fresh new angle from him. He didn't back down, and neither did I.

My stubbornness means I missed out on one of the biggest names for both an article and the all-important cover lines to attract sales to a brand-new magazine. But it also meant that I did not bend on my values, which I think is an imperative in business and, indeed, life.

And as I mentioned earlier, I didn't go into business purely to make money, so I definitely don't make decisions about my business based purely on the potential financial outcome. As a business grows and matures, people often want to know whether you plan to stay or whether you'll create a succession plan and leave, but (for me anyway) my business is absolutely about more than that.

I have been amazed at how many times people have asked me what my exit strategy is. Of course I get it, I totally do—but this isn't just about money or moving on to the next big project. It comes back to my sense of purpose.

We interviewed a creative genius for the magazine just after our first birthday, and as part of the interview, he said he'd fended off three offers to buy his business in the last six months alone. He wasn't the least bit interested, but explained, "This is my life's work; I don't want to just give it to anyone." I couldn't have agreed more.

Some people may think my motivation for creating the magazine was to eventually sell to the big boys we had fought against for shelf space in the early days, and while that could happen (I'm an open-minded person), it was never my intention to do so. I would have happily sold the book arm of the business, but it was largely tied to me and so not exactly scalable.

However, when it comes to the magazine—which has now developed into a rather large, platform-agnostic movement, as was always the intention—I unequivocally believe I am on purpose, and as a result, there isn't enough money in the world to drag me away from it.

When the idea of the magazine had just begun, a partner at a major law firm (and a good friend) had coffee with me to share some news: He was leaving the firm and exploring other options. He wondered if I wanted to head up an online book distribution company. His checkbook open, he looked straight at me.

In that moment, I knew no amount of money could keep me from moving ahead with the magazine. After all, I was being offered an incredible opportunity—with all the support and financial backing that an entrepreneur dreams of—and it didn't even pique my interest.

When you cry out for purpose and find it, why would you throw it away so quickly—or for something as invaluable as money? Yes, money is a nice by-product of a thriving business and helps with platform and scale, but isn't the greater meaning in doing something that you absolutely love, that you feel so aligned with that you just can't wait to jump out of bed every day to do it?

If I had $10 million or even $100 million, that wouldn't buy me happiness. It might buy me a nice lifestyle. But I'm an entrepreneur. I want to do cool stuff. I want to make a difference. So even with all that money in the bank, I'd still be left sitting there again, asking the universe, "What next?"

BE DETACHED FROM OUTCOME

If you feel you have found your purpose, it becomes easier to be detached from day-to-day situations that may or may not go to plan. Because you are aware of the bigger picture, you know that it's okay to deviate along the way and you are undeterred when things don't go exactly to plan.

Detaching yourself from specific outcomes isn't always easy—in fact, for an overachieving former control freak like me, it's a big call—but it is possible. It means that you can have dreams and ideas and you chase them wholeheartedly, but if they don't work out or don't go exactly as you had planned, you can chose to move on quickly and try something else, heart still intact. Ultimately, after all, the aim is to succeed in business and make a mark on the world; the details of exactly how that plays out aren't important.

The notion of detachment from outcome is a relatively new one for me, although I've probably been actively and consciously practicing it for a few years, and doing it on a subconscious level for years before that. I simply didn't put a label on it or write it down as a business technique to conquer (ironically, because I like those!).

What it has meant is a shift in the way I address ideas (completely open, but not obsessed), as well as noticeably less fear (almost negligible) about whether something will succeed.

People often put together an extensive business plan—I'm talking thick dossiers that they've labored over for weeks, months, or even years. Then they start building prototypes and designing websites in preparation for launch. And all that time, effort, and money has often been spent before they've even found out if there is a willing market or willing and interested investors.

We can become extraordinarily attached to our specific end game, product, or service—so much so that it becomes our entire focus. That's completely understandable—I mean, what kind of entrepreneur doesn't get caught up in his or her own hype and excitement at one point or another?

The problem with this, however, is that the wheels could fall off, and if you're too focused on your goal to see the storm brewing around you, your journey could be over before it truly began.

Trust me when I say that the wheels can fall off in dozens of different ways. Perhaps there's no market, or the market was ready twelve months ago and you missed it. Or maybe the market will be ready in twelve months time and you're too early. You might not have the cash needed to build momentum, or the staff you hired doesn't work out, or you can't get something manufactured as you had hoped. All of these scenarios can easily happen.

And when they do, someone who has invested an immense amount into a particular outcome is often deeply disheartened and no longer has the passion, energy, time, soul, self-esteem, or anything else to continue on. That's when many people start to see themselves as failures, and the thought of giving up is as ever present as the air they breathe.

The thing is, they're not failures: They've just invested every last drop of their being into an idea, leaving them completely sapped of life.

If you have an idea, the best place to start is always right there—with the idea. You may actually have loads of them. Scribble down the top-level essence of what you want to do. Then if you are a good networker, you'll have a whole host of fabulous corporate types or individuals with spare cash who might be able to help you fund your project. If you have great relationships, you can quickly bounce these ideas past them. If an idea has some stickiness (in other words, you attract some interest), then you can develop it a little further.

Being detached from specific outcomes is about relinquishing control and surrendering. There is a wonderful saying known as the Serenity Prayer that has been a mantra I have called on daily for a good part of the last ten years: "Grant me the serenity to accept the things I cannot change, the courage to change the things I can, and the wisdom to know the difference."

Control is the sense of security you have as a result of being attached to a specific outcome that you have predetermined is best. Once you're able to start to trust that whatever happens, you will be okay, you can stop micromanaging your every move and that of the greater universe—and instead let go, have some fun, and slip into the groove.

Think about a time when you have just handed something over. Things just seem to automatically run more smoothly. It's pointless to use energy planning, predicting, or trying to control things that can't be planned, predicted, or controlled.

As soon as I let go of the notion of how I think something should run, things just seem to work and situations that I never imagined were possible start opening up and appearing. And whenever I have doggedly pursued some specific, predetermined outcomes I've had in mind, more often than not, the scenario plays out much smaller than it could have.

Now, this is not to say I just wake up, sit on my bed, and wait for the world to miraculously bestow positive outcomes and happiness upon me. I set my intentions and have a strong set of values and beliefs and a greater purpose. It just means I am not attached to the specifics of the outcome. This enables me to morph, pivot, change, and adapt to whatever happens to roll.

You will start to notice that the energy of surrender takes way less energy than the energy of control. I can feel myself slipping into a calmer, more relaxed, nimble, free-flowing state when I am consciously there.

Whereas when I am trying to control things, I am pent-up, anxious, and overbearing. It's not a pleasant state and I am certainly not productive: I have little awareness of the present, my concentration is poor, and my brain is more erratic than usual. The irony can often be that the more you try to control things, the more out of control you feel.

The art of surrender means to stop fighting—with yourself, with others, with the universe—and to let it go. It doesn't mean take no action, but rather, take action from a place of surrendered, gentler energy.

FIND your
PURPOSE
change the
WORLD
BE AUTHENTIC
BE A LEADER
BE YOU
TRAVEL
for inspiration

PLAY A BIG GAME

get CREATIVE

ALLOW yourself to get

MAD

surrender

FAIL FAST

When I left school, I felt driven to make my own way in the world. Even as a teenager, I had this absolute, inherent yearning to do things against the grain. "I don't want a cent," I told my mum as I packed for a gap year in England after completing my final year of schooling.

As we arrived at Sydney International Airport, my mom handed me a package of throat lozenges and gave me a hug, and that was it for almost two years. I think she took me a little too literally when I proclaimed I could do it all on my own, but as it turns out, I could. With a pack on my back, I headed off and did exactly as I planned, first working as a pony trekking instructor earning £35 a week—which was essentially enough for beer—and it worked out okay, because the job came with free accommodations and food.

Two years later, I was in Rome with my boyfriend at the time when the van we had managed to buy on the cheap was vandalized, and all of our worldly possessions were stolen while we were swimming at the beach. They took my money, clothes, toiletries, and journal—everything, including my return ticket home.

Fortunately I had my passport strapped around my waist while we were at the beach. I walked into the police station (the words *carabinieri*, the national police of Italy, and *polizia* stuck with me for years afterward) in my bikini, and they came running from everywhere, waving their hands and saying I couldn't be in there without clothes on.

"But I have nothing!" I cried, so they interviewed me outside of the station. When I spoke to my dad about the situation, he went into a mild panic and said I needed to come home immediately. My answer was so quick, it was almost involuntary: "Absolutely no way. I'll work it out," I said.

So we hitchhiked to the coast of Brindisi, in the south of Italy, and got on a boat (I'm not sure if we paid for our passage—quite possibly it was an illegal move, as we slept on the deck overnight). We ended up in Piraeus, Greece.

Having been fired from a casual job at KFC a few years earlier for my poor waitressing skills, I must have had some serious cojones to walk into a German-owned restaurant run by a Greek guy with a chef from New York and a very English front of house, but I did. That's how I ended up pulling beers, agreeing to learn Greek on the fly. I worked for as long as it took to buy a ticket home. A few months after being robbed, I was on a flight home to Sydney.

People always say I was a very determined soul—I'm hard to knock down and much harder to keep down—and now that I reflect on it, I can see that this attitude has held me in good stead for business. The entrepreneurial journey is really one big conglomerate of challenges to overcome, fears to face, failure to endure, and—the big prize at the end—success to enjoy, in whatever form that may take.

Failure is a huge area of interest for entrepreneurs, understandably so. For the uninitiated, *failure* can seem like a dirty word, one with negative connotations. But it is an essential element of business and life, and one that can actually be your friend, if you let it. No matter how good you are, you can't avoid failing sometimes. And as you grow, you'll have mishaps and more significant failures that happen as a result of elements outside of your control.

There's the small stuff, the mishaps and missteps. These are the meetings where you fall flat, the presentations you mess up, the clients you fail to land for one reason or another.

There are the moments you wish you could take back—when your cat poops in the potted plant in the corner while you're midway through an important client meeting, for instance (yes, this happened, and fortunately, the client didn't notice because he had his back to the cat). Or when your intern serves a potentially high-value client a cup of tea in a mug that still bears the price tag of a secondhand store (I was hoping they thought it was a creative Japanese motif).

Then there are the slightly more significant setbacks. I recall discovering that we'd sent a client's book off to the printer with duplicated pages, and another time, the color matching was all wrong: The person on the cover looked as if he'd drunk a gallon of carrot juice. Sadly, that book needed a reprint. There are system failures, too, and we've had a few of those.

When we interviewed the model, actress, and entrepreneur Kathy Ireland in New York for the magazine, she made this profound statement: "Allow people to refute you, but never allow them to dismiss you. Look at failure as education."

Fortunately, in all my years in business (touch wood), we haven't had too many significant failures. I think that's largely because we've always moved quickly, adapted, thought on our feet, been proactive, and failed fast. What we have had is a string of smaller failures that have pushed us forward, providing knowledge and wisdom. I am constantly amazed at my own staff and know they are part of the reason for this. Whenever there is a problem or potential problem, they are always positive and solution-driven; they don't dwell on things or get angry. It's a great culture to have and has been key to reducing the number of business-wide failures or difficult situations we have had.

I think the key to failure is that if you're going to fail, you may as well do it fast. I have seen so many people do it ridiculously slowly and painfully. It kills me every time to watch someone experience great personal and professional grief over many months or even years. I've never really failed slowly, probably because I'm too impatient for that.

If I'm going to fail, then I want to do it well—fast and with minimum risk. And as a result of this ethos, I'm quite prepared to try out a lot of new and interesting things, unafraid of the outcome. The traditional mind-set is to write a laborious business plan to perfection, run a zillion focus groups, do all your market research, and check every conceivable box before launching into something, but I rarely (okay, never . . . yet) do that.

To take that approach requires a huge investment of time, resources, and money, and you are already deep into the project's life cycle before you even know if someone is going to buy what you're selling. And by the time you launch, you've perfected your idea to within an inch of its life, so when the market gives you feedback, it's often too late to change, move, and adapt. Instead, the experience can leave you feeling paralyzed by disappointment and with a sense of hopelessness about pursuing other ideas.

Setbacks are just that – they set you back.

So FAIL FAST and move on with warp speed.

Don't get me wrong—I do my due diligence, but just not to the point that the poor project is suffocated or strangled before we even begin.

Take the *Collective Hub*™ magazine, for instance. I didn't do any business plans. I did a little market research, and once I confirmed that there was nothing like this already out there, I kicked into high gear and began taking action toward making the magazine a reality.

In truth, I thought the model would be very different from what it is today. I really thought we would presell copies to corporates, as per our book model, and that newsstand sales would comprise 3 to 5 percent of the market. This being the case, my due diligence was focused around working out whom to presell to.

It wasn't really until we began meeting with distributors and I realized how excited they were that we began exploring other options. Keep in mind that these were the people who distribute esteemed, proven titles that have been in the market for decades. And they were begging to take us on? That's when I started to see that we could be an equally serious player in this space. Doors just kept opening up from there.

Of course, that's not to say I take every idea I have and pursue it with reckless abandon! It's no stretch to say that entrepreneurs will come up with a hundred or more business ideas in a year; that's less than two decent ideas a week, which seems more than fair. The ideas are not always viable, but they're always showing up. They come from listening and watching everywhere you go, and being open to the opportunities that you find along the way.

And they can stem from your own needs or from observing markets around you.

I tend to sit on a new idea and examine it in my head. I try to gauge my level of interest and overall passion, asking myself if I have the sweat and tears to pour into it, because I know that's what will be needed should I decide to do this. In other words, you need to be really juiced up and passionate about it, or it will never fly.

If I feel the idea has wings, I generally write up a few pages on it—literally back-of-the-envelope stuff, things such as an overview, indicative model, potential markets, and indicative marketing/launch, so that I have something to test out with potential partners.

It can happen within an hour to a week of the birth of the idea, and if I get a bite, I investigate further and start to make more concrete plans. But if I discover that no one is interested, then I bop it on the head, moving on to something else. Pretty simple, really. I do this over and over and over again. It is the only way I work. I never plan more than this initially. And as it grows, you can look at extension ideas and test them out in the same way.

A friend of mine was recently deliberating on his next business. A few quick questions from me and a few short answers from him were as follows:

ME: What are you passionate about at the moment?
HIM: Travel and food.
ME: Where, specifically?
HIM: Bali.

ME: Would you like to run foodie tours?

HIM: That would be amazing.

Now, at this point, most people would run off and write said business plan, evaluate it, cost out all the options, and plan the next steps. But what I say and what I do each and every time is some form of quick market testing.

So I simply said to him: "Choose a social media platform and post right now, 'Who's interested in doing a foodie tour to Bali with me?'"

Honestly, it can be that simple. I might choose to throw it out to my social media platforms, it might be in the form of an email or call to a potential corporate partner, it might be a face-to-face meeting—it depends on the idea. But it is fast.

Now, coming back to the foodie tours in Bali. Let's say my friend followed my advice and threw that question up on Twitter. If that's the case, it's out there now. Once people start showing interest and a few replies come back saying, "Yep, sounds great; I'd love to know more"—that's when he should start to develop the materials, look at the costs, and begin to navigate the logistics, and not a moment earlier.

So the next thing my friend might go back with is, "Okay, it's going to run over five days. It will include all meals and will cost about three thousand dollars." If people are still interested and he has ten people who are still keen to know more, then he has the start of a business.

I do things this way because it allows me to pursue an idea

incrementally, depending on response, so that I don't have to do the hard, time-consuming, costly work until I have the cold hard cash on the line. It's a way to tackle new ideas and provides the opportunity to "fail" before the situation becomes too complicated.

As an entrepreneur, it means you can build things as the market reacts; you can even build them once you know they are almost presold. This is where the gold is. So the key lesson is to listen to your market and respond accordingly—and quickly.

People think there's a quick fix out there for business success. I've failed over and over and over again, and when you fail that many times, something finally sticks. Failure is another word for experience. So when the topic of failure pops up, with all its (normally) nasty connotations, I'm quick to say I don't mind it. From this you can see how quickly and often I can let myself fail.

Who wants to fail, right? Me. A lot. Because it makes me stronger, teaches me loads, and reminds me that I'm only human. It also propels me forward, and that's exactly the direction I want to be going in. And while there are setbacks, they do just that: They set you back a bit and then you get going again, back on the path to awesomeness. As Facebook founder Mark Zuckerberg says, "The biggest risk is not taking any risk. . . . In a world that's changing really quickly, the only strategy that is guaranteed to fail is not taking risks."

FAIL FAST

TAKE RISKS

Push the boundaries

START BEFORE you're ready.

JUST GO

DON'T
WALLOW
GROW & MOVE ON
FAILURE
can be your
FRIEND.
THE world
is yours

DREAM BIG, DREAM OFTEN

Many years ago, on a rooftop in Marrakesh, Morocco, I sat and scribbled down initial ideas (read: a sketchy business plan) for a series of magazines I could develop. This was years before I started the *Collective Hub*™, which was clearly an idea that had been bubbling away for quite some time.

Amid the sound of the leather tannery workers busily doing their thing below and the intermittent clacking of a donkey's hooves on the adjacent cobblestone lane, I relaxed and got lost in my thoughts. The afternoon call to prayer was just beginning to sound, and with the sun on my face and a cup of ridiculously sweet mint tea in my hand, I began to dream.

Ostensibly I was in Morocco to relax and switch off, although entrepreneurs know there is no such thing. I'd just spent two busy weeks pitching books to international buyers at the Frankfurt Book Fair. But Morocco was alive with activity and culture that sent my mind into a spin. It was a crazy, chaotic experience—at one point, a male traveling buddy was offered two camels in exchange for the "big one," which was me (gulp, time to lay off the tagines)—and as a result I was buzzing with millions of possibilities.

"There is one thing stronger than all the armies in the world," says the poet Victor Hugo, "and that is an idea whose time has come." My idea's time hadn't come just yet; this was 2007, and I didn't launch the magazine until 2013. But the seeds were being well and truly planted.

And while I knew that the magazine idea wasn't for now, I felt it had merit and would allow me to build the life I wanted and make the impact I had hoped for. The *Collective Hub*™ as it stands today is a completely different beast from the type of magazine I thought I'd produce, but that evening still stands out for me. It was my first foray into exploring this idea and would be a sign of things to come—my "sketchy" business plan was penned among the rooftop cushions, plants, and satellite dishes!

A year later, back home and extremely busy with the book business, which had really hit its stride by this point in time, I decided to register a business name around magazines. Two years after that, I bought a book entitled *How to Start a Magazine*.

As I look back at these three events, it's clear to me that the idea of a magazine had been subconsciously brewing for a while, although I hadn't really joined the dots until I looked back over my journals.

But it wasn't until March 2012 that I began to take this idea more seriously. One Monday morning I walked into the office, called a team meeting, and said with absolute certainty, "I think we should launch a magazine." Within seconds (quite literally), we started writing back-of-the-envelope sales materials.

The day before, we'd had a focus meeting in which we had decided unequivocally that we were not going to deviate from the business of books. In fact, we weren't even going to try to do extensions from books of any kind, which were pretty lucrative but also time-consuming. No, we would do only books, 100 percent. Books. Just books.

But I went home that night and had a topsy-turvy fight-with-the-bedcovers kind of night. The notion of books alone rolled over in my brain. It just wasn't right. It was fine, but fine was not enough. The idea of the magazine resurfaced and kept forcing itself into my thinking like an insolent child.

I just kept mulling it over in my brain, so much so that when I walked into my office the next morning, I couldn't keep from sharing it with my freshly focused team. They may have been thinking books, but the only thing on my brain was my magazine idea. Thankfully, all of my staff at the time (a total of three) jumped up with excitement and said they were in. Only one thought we were all mad, and she cried buckets at the launch twelve months later, saying she couldn't quite believe that we had actually done it.

That, in a nutshell, is the magazine's journey: from the speck of an idea on a rooftop in Marrakesh many years ago, to now being a global force, distributed in over thirty countries and growing.

That's the thing about ideas. Most of us entrepreneurs have a continuous flow of them. Perhaps that's why most of the entrepreneurs I know are a little offbeat: crazy, wild, undisciplined, and unfocused. Their minds buzz about everything from the shaver they just used that didn't work very well ("I will design a better shaver!" they exclaim) to the designer label they saw overseas that isn't available in their own nation yet ("Fashion—I could do fashion," they muse) to an export business they hear of in a noncompeting industry ("I should meet with them and get an idea of how we could work together . . .").

They see ideas in everyone and everything. And the dire point is that they must do exactly that—keep the ideas flowing, for it's in those times of craziness and inspiration that some of the best ones are formed.

As entrepreneurs, we must let ourselves dream even if everyone else around us (sane or otherwise) thinks that our ideas are ridiculous—too simple, too complex, or too boring; that we are too young or too old to achieve them; and so on and so on. Spend some time teaching yourself to dream with your eyes open, if you don't already, even in the room you are sitting in right now. Look at the walls, what's on the table or the floor—there will be hundreds of opportunities for inspiration if you look hard enough.

We must also expect ideas to come from strange places. As I have said, my first book, *Happiness Is . . .* , came from a time of deep personal searching, but the very first idea, the notion of even doing a book, came from a few hours spent with a couple of builders.

I'd always worked in the service industry, where you do something for others instead of creating a product to sell to market. Yet by some strange connection through another client, I was invited to the pilot of the TV show *The New Inventors.*

There I met a couple of guys who had invented a dump plate, which is basically a plate that builders bolt to the top of toilets on construction sites to stop people taking a dump in unplumbed toilets. Sorry for the visual—not pretty, but true, and it was a major problem for the industry.

I ended up doing some consultancy for them and got quite excited about the potential (what can I say? When I get excited and see potential in something, my enthusiasm knows no bounds!), but that was when I started to think that I needed a product of my own. From a dump plate, the ideas began to flow.

I considered golf fashion, because poorly fitting knee-length beige culottes (there is no other word to describe that tragedy) weren't doing it for me on the golf course. I lost interest in pursuing that line of thought and quickly moved into gardening. With a penchant for potting, I was soon introduced to the power of self-propagating plants.

I discovered a product called rooting gel, which enables you to start a bunch of new plants using just the clippings from another. I called them money trees, because each sprout could become a new plant to sell. I started buying quirky pots from secondhand stores and thought I'd sell my own self-rooting, self-propagating money plants.

That idea fizzled, so I began wondering if you could remelt the wax that drips down the side of burning candles so none was wasted. Then I was on to soap, wondering what happens to the soap in hotel rooms that the guests use for one (two, max) showers. Where does it go, and what could be done with that? After any unwanted hairs were removed, surely you could do something of value with that soap.

And then I stumbled across a book—a better, more world-changing proposition than hair-free repurposed soap.

Some of the best ideas come from experiencing a pain point or seeing a problem for yourself or others that needs a solution. The easiest and most simple thing to do is to jump into the shoes of the customer and genuinely put yourself in his or her position by thinking, "What do I need?"

That's why so often you see ideas born out of situations like "I had a baby and there was no natural, safe diaper cream that actually worked" or "I was a left-handed dentist and there were no tools designed specifically for dentists like me."

When you put yourself in the shoes of the consumer, you find out what the world needs so you can create it. I think what happens is that this often plays out the other way around. People come up with great ideas and then implement them, without first really examining if there is a market.

I once heard about a serial entrepreneur through a friend. This guy is a real go-getter, the type of person who always has a dozen businesses in various stages of development. One day, many years ago, he had an idea to create an online appointment system for the restaurant industry.

The idea of booking a table at a restaurant online might seem pretty par for the course now, but it's actually a relatively new thing. This was back in 2007, so restaurants weren't as tech-smart or consumer-savvy as they are now; in fact, some didn't even have a website (the horror!). Back then, you'd pick up the phone and, you know, call a restaurant to make a booking. Crazy, I know.

He thought an online booking system was a great idea, but he needed to know if consumers agreed with him. So he took his idea to the market and tested it.

One Wednesday, he stood on a city corner during the busy lunch hour and stopped strangers on the street. He asked them two quick questions: "Would you make a restaurant reservation online if you could? And would you be willing to pay for the service?"

Three hours and 250 surveys later, he had his answer: a resounding and enthusiastic yes. People wanted the convenience and ease of making a restaurant booking online. But they weren't prepared to pay for it.

His next step was to go to restaurants for their feedback. He was pleased to learn that this would address a concern in their business. They explained that they didn't have the manpower to handle phone bookings during the busy lunch rush, which was usually when people called to make reservations for dinner. As a result, many restaurants were losing valuable bookings. So not only were they keen on the idea, but they were willing to pay for it.

As it turns out, his idea did meet a very real need in the market, but not in the way he expected. He thought he was creating a valuable service for consumers, but the pain point for them was really quite minimal. When you're booking a restaurant, it's not a big deal to call the restaurant if you can't book online.

But a restaurant owner who is losing money due to an inability to answer reservation inquiries during the lunch hour? That is a customer who has a genuine problem.

When you think about your idea, can you come up with at least a dozen compelling pain points it addresses? Will it make someone's life or business easier, more convenient, more profitable, or more fulfilled? These are the kinds of questions you need to ask.

If you don't have an idea yet, don't despair; there are plenty of world-changing, groundbreaking discoveries yet to be made. You may think everything has been done before, but there are many unmet needs in this complex world. The *Collective Hub*™ has certainly been an example of that.

In Australia alone there are over 5,000 print magazines. I was once told that we produce more magazines per capita here than in any other developed nation in the world. So who would have thought in a "dying, antiquated market" such as magazine publishing, there would be room for another?

Yet, there was a need. A market gap just waiting for someone to fill it. And I was more than ready to step up and bridge the gap.

Don't beat yourself up if you can't seem to come up with the perfect idea straightaway. As I mentioned earlier, the idea for the *Collective Hub*™ was in the hopper for years, even if I didn't recognize it at the time.

When it comes to ideas, you also need to give yourself permission to dream big. Really big. Get your idea and make it as big as you possibly can in your mind, not worrying about the money.

That's one of the secrets to really taking the lid off the pot: You need to absolutely remove the "lack of money" barrier from your head if you want to truly create a game-changing, market-disrupting idea. Instead, you must completely go into the mind-set of "If I had all the money in the world, how would I do it?" That way you can get really clear on where you want to go—and once you get excited about that, more often than not, the money has a way of coming.

Always go to the big, visionary, dreamy picture first, and then work back to figure out how you are going to make it happen. Approaching it this way removes all barriers and eliminates concerns about the infrastructure you'll need. That's where you should be taking it, and that's where you need to let your mind wander.

When I decided to launch a magazine, I wanted it to be BIG from the start. I wasn't at all interested in playing a small game, so if I was going to do this thing, I was going to do it well. We had dabbled in offshore distribution with books, but had never achieved it with any great success, despite a few decent attempts—including one push in New York City where we secured thirty-one meetings in five days—but I just didn't have what it took at the time to pull it off. We didn't have the grunt behind us to get the momentum we needed.

With the magazine, I wanted to dig deep and tap into this grunt from the get-go. I was so hungry for change that I didn't have anything to lose. As a result, I let my mind run wild, and this situation proved that when you really let yourself shoot for the stars, you can actually reach some of them.

I signed the lease on a new office that could house more than eight times the staff I had at the time. If I was going to do this, I was damn well going to jump in boots and all and make as big and as positive an impact as I possibly could. I wasn't good at doing anything halfheartedly.

DREAM BIG,
DREAM OFTEN

Let your
subconscious run

wild

LOOK for
INSPIRATION
everywhere

accept
CRAZY
IDEAS
MAKE
your
DREAMS
come true.

Did I realize just how big it would go? Probably not even close, but the intention was there and it was set into me like concrete. I kept saying to my mum, "It's going to be big." Poor mum—I think I nearly drove her nuts. When the physical magazine landed and she and my sister saw it in our office on the day of the launch, they said, "Wow, it's a real magazine." Yes, it was.

I remember in my launch speech—pretty ballsy in hindsight—I made a very loud and very purposeful statement about how we were going to change the face of the media landscape and really shake things up. I said this with as much confidence as I had in me to a crowd of over two hundred of the smartest minds in this country. I backed myself with every bit of nerve and guts and gumption I had in me. How on earth did I know how much traction it would have early on?

I didn't. But I let myself dream that it would. I had to. I had to live and breathe it. Out loud. Authentically.

People ask me how I am making a difference or sharing. I am doing it the only way I know how: leading by example. By being an entrepreneur for entrepreneurs who isn't afraid to let herself dream and, more important, do.

And that leads me into the next part of idea creation. If you are going to dream, then bloody well get out there and do something with it. You don't have to follow every idea. In fact that would be ridiculous, and if I had taken that stance, I'd have a mildly successful dripping wax company instead of a growing global multimedia movement. But you need to do something with some of them.

There are two types of people in this world—the implementers and the gunnas. The gunnas always say they're gunna do this and gunna do that, but really, they never do. So no matter how good their idea is, it will always be just an idea.

I love the implementers, those who put their butts on the line and commit. They reach inside themselves and get a little uncomfortable, because at the end of the day, they get out there and do.

There are two
types of
people
out there
—the "implementers"
and the
"gunnas".

Don't be
a gunna!

CULTURE
UP

The day I started writing this chapter, I had a meeting with my deputy editor in the front seat of her car while one of her kids slept in the back (the other was furiously scarfing dry breakfast cereal and squirting black-currant juice at me).

I had told the office I was popping down to the car for a chat, and three other staffers also had things to discuss with her, so they decided they would come. While I sat in the front with the windows rolled down, they stood on the street and we talked through the issues and had a few laughs—and cups of coffee from the café next door—in between.

This was a typical afternoon of *Collective Hub*™ madness. Honestly, we're all over the place, but in the most perfectly productive and organized way. I don't run my office on a nine-to-five clock (thank god—some of our best ideas and achievements happen early in the morning or late at night, when the rest of the world is resting), and there are always people coming and going, meeting here or there, trying this product and testing that website.

We will often crowd around one person's desk to check out the latest social media fad or trending story. And it's not uncommon to see one of our team members shuffling down the street walking my dog, Benny; in fact one of our design team trotted past with Benny during our roadside powwow.

I view my employees as my work family—I certainly spend more time with them than I do with my actual relatives—so I think it's important that we have a great time when we're together. We work hard, undoubtedly. But I deliberately and purposefully invest time and energy into cultivating a positive work culture, so that our office is a place people genuinely want to be.

The way I see it, your culture and your people are the absolute backbone of your business. They can make or break you internally and are your flagship to the world outside. Once a business owner creates a personal and company brand identity, a corporate culture is the next most important thing, as it's intrinsically linked with your brand. Those who have gallantly pioneered it (Google, Facebook, and the like) have proven this in spades, and it's not rocket science. I found my head nodding in agreement when I saw these words from the legendary entrepreneur and thought leader Tom Peters, who said, "The simple act of paying positive attention to people has a great deal to do with productivity."

Before my business opened, I knew I wanted a very purposeful culture: a fun, warm place that people loved getting up and coming to every day, that had the feel of a family, and where our hard work would be rewarded with limitless opportunity. In essence, I wanted to create the type of energetic, inspirational workplace where the mantra "Anything is possible" would fill our heads.

When you spend that much of your week with the same group of people and in the same place, you want it to be good. Fantastic, even. For them, but also for you.

If you're working long hours consistently or revving it up at key times (there were plenty of all-nighters when the magazine launched—thanks, team), then you can easily spend more time with your workmates in a week than you do with your own partners, family, and friends in a month.

It's imperative that you make that time spent together productive and efficient for the company, but also deeply rewarding for every person there. While we don't always get it right, we strive for it every day, the aim being to make our workplace a family environment and where possible to work with people of similar values.

Getting your culture right is crucial to your professional success. It requires that you have a vision and that you deliberately put things in place to achieve it. It means hiring the right people and (sadly) ensuring that the wrong ones leave as quickly and as painlessly as possible. It also means leading by example and stamping out any bad behavior or possible culture killers as they arrive.

If your culture also equals your brand, then in building an extraordinary culture, you will be automatically and organically building an extraordinary brand. The opposite, therefore, can also happen. The values of your organization need to stem and flow from your personal brand values as the leader, and this naturally and authentically creates consistency and congruency within your staff.

Internally, if your team loves your culture, then their output will be significantly greater than that of disengaged employees. From an external perspective, the world will gravitate toward you and your team, attracted to its vibe, positivity, and success, because great culture automatically creates flow and momentum.

When it comes to hiring staff, I'm fussy, and we now have a culture that is equally fussy. For the most part, we hire on passion, attitude, and cultural fit over experience and skill every single time, because skill is the easiest thing to teach people and experience we can give—but rewiring a person's attitude or digging for passion is far harder!

My approach has always been to hire my weaknesses. (Side point: I absolutely love this advice from the business consultant Jim Collins: "You absolutely must have the discipline not to hire until you find the right people.") If I hired people just like me, we would end up with an insanely visionary workplace containing all the ideas in the world, but no one detail-oriented enough to turn all of our dreams into plans.

I'm also not interested in people who just want a job. I can sniff out if a candidate just wants some experience before moving on to a (perceived) bigger, better opportunity in twelve months, wasting his time and ours in the process.

Instead, I actively recruit people who are passionate and proactive, people who have no ego and no problem pitching in, whatever the task of the day requires.

Practically, I love to bring people into the fold on a casual basis before we make the jump and offer them full-time employment. This is not always possible, but it's the approach we take whenever we can. I love to test them technically before they join our team and also to see if they can work under pressure, if they'll fit in with the existing crew and make it a better place, not a more difficult one. I question how open they are, how much self-discovery they've done, how self-aware they are, how much emotional intelligence they have, and how willing and open they are to develop. Closed minds don't pass go.

Despite all of my best intentions, many times the culture has been wrong and rapid correction was needed. Early in the magazine's life, I hired way too quickly and didn't have the right mix of people or the right people in the right jobs. As a result, we had to let some people go and restructure internally to get back on track. They were competent people as individuals, but the mix wasn't right at the time. The "hire slowly, fire quickly" mantra is key.

I also realize that start-ups are not for everyone. Entrepreneurs are crazy beings. We have a zillion ideas, and the frenetic, million-miles-an-hour energy that this creates in a workplace is not for everyone. People may come in and start working on one job, and as the company morphs and changes, they may have to take on a completely different role. I need them to be able to adapt.

If you work with entrepreneurs, you will rarely find yourself in a nine-to-five role and no two days will ever be the same. There is often little order (especially early on), and there are few defined systems or documented processes. You are thrown in and will often have to create things on the fly, gaining experience as you go; if you don't swim, you will sink.

It takes a certain kind of leader to be able to get people to buy into the visions created and a certain type of person to be able to work in this environment. But when it works, extraordinary things can be achieved very quickly. This is the joy of being nimble, adaptable, and open to opportunities and change.

I have always let opportunity be my biggest weapon. One of the best things you can offer an employee is the ability to dream, but also the support to get there. You might not always be able to pay them big dollars (in the early days), but opportunity can be of equal value.

When we were pounding the pavement before the *Collective Hub*™ was launched, we met with a wonderful luxury brand, which we hoped would come on board as an advertising partner. We were chatting about the design. The person we were meeting with was enthusiastic and asked, "Who have you got art directing? Are you flying someone in from Paris, London, or New York City?" As if these were the only options.

My mind flashed to the cramped back room of our office, where my then twenty-two-year-old designer—who started out as an intern and was first employed as a project manager for the book side of our business—was thrashing out the design concepts for our first issue. Without hesitation, I replied, "No, I have one of the best designers available in Australia."

And I wasn't lying. She's an incredible designer and I couldn't be prouder to have her on our team. She had natural raw talent and could think laterally across all parts of the company. She was exactly what we needed, and in return, we would give her the world in terms of experience and opportunity.

It's important to recognize and nurture good talent and believe in yourself and those around you. In my book, passion and loyalty win out over experience every single time.

Whether you own a company or are a part of it, you can still have an entrepreneurial spirit pumping through your veins.

I am also a huge believer in fostering entrepreneurialism within our company. I always say to my staff that they should dream big, asking them where they want to be in one, two, or five years time.

If they tell me they want to run their own businesses one day, I tell them to practice within our philosophy of "go for it: come up with ideas and come back to me with a proposal as to how we can achieve it." If there's merit in their idea and it fits with our values and makes commercial sense, I will back them 100 percent and be willing to invest the time and money into making it happen.

Or if they want to work overseas, then my attitude is, let's work out a way for them to run an arm of the business offshore. If they want to move up to a more senior role, then let's put a plan in place to test them, build up their skills, and train them to fill their new pair of shoes.

We say "dream big" and we mean it, because if you let people be intrapreneurial (entrepreneurs within a company), you'll find that they rarely leave, or at the very least, you'll get the best from them while they're with you, and they'll gain a wealth of experience and opportunity to take into the next phase of their life.

When people see that culture in action, their thinking will change, affecting their day-to-day behavior. They'll look up and out more often, and they'll see small obstacles as exactly what they are—hindrances to be overcome—rather than becoming paralyzed when challenges come their way. They'll believe in their ideas, build arguments for them, and challenge the status quo because they're living in a working environment that does exactly the same thing.

At the same time, you have to be strategic about what you throw at a staff member and think long-term about their future career with you or another company. I once gave an eighteen-year-old the title of business development manager, which went south very quickly. Her behavior changed, and I quickly discovered that while she had all of the potential in the world, she didn't have the attitude, skills, or time in the game to back it up.

In the end, she left, and I knew she needed to. I had unwittingly helped facilitate an out-of-control ego. She is an incredibly talented person and I have no doubt she will make a massive mark on the world! It was just another lesson for me—give people opportunities, but never put the cart before the horse; let them walk before they run.

Part of building a strong, cohesive culture is about leading big. By that I mean you must continuously talk about the big picture. It's your job to create a vision that everyone feels a part of and then to empower them to carry out their contribution. Educate them on the bigger picture and keep them in the loop about what you are all working so hard and so passionately toward.

You need to help them feel a part of something bigger, a greater community, and keep communicating to everyone about their part in the company. When we were working on the first issue of the magazine, I was acutely aware that the only way to get out the first edition (it was pretty touch and go as we bumbled along) was to continually remind the team of the bigger picture and to encourage them daily (even hourly when times got tough), telling them that I believed in them and that if we were successful, it meant a new future for everyone.

They needed it because they worked long hours (some slept in the office on multiple occasions) and gave up their weekends and holidays for months before launch. Essentially the office became our new home. They also jumped into any role necessary and didn't complain; they just got in and did it. Together.

Then you must look at personal motivations and reward accordingly. Where some leaders go wrong is when they stick to a rigid, "one size fits all" approach to team management. Everyone is motivated by different things—some by money, others by title, recognition, key performance indicators or goals, and so forth.

I try to get to the source of people's motivations and work with them accordingly. One day I popped a check for $200 on the desk of a staff member who I knew wanted a new pair of leather boots for winter. That same day I enrolled another staff member in a course that would propel her career—and her knowledge base within our company—massively forward. Another time I agreed to buy a gorgeous pet office bunny, Bosley, for a team member.

The results for all—while drastically different in approach and different in cost, I might add—were the same. All three were instantly grateful, encouraged, and motivated and felt valued for their efforts.

Among every team I've ever had, there has always been a mix of personalities and motivations. A new title can be worth more to some people than a raise in pay.

Likewise, consistent education, training, and the opportunity to attend the latest industry events will be worth more than a new title for some. Others will be more interested in the freedom of wearing whatever they want and the ability to have pets roaming through our offices than in whether or not we're making the big bucks.

On a practical level, there are many things you can do to create a kick-ass culture. You can let people be themselves and wear what they want to promote freedom and self-expression. You can create a family atmosphere by having regular team lunches and outings or Friday-afternoon drinks, by celebrating birthdays and special events. (I once made my staff meet me in the mall and I gave them each an envelope of cash for their Christmas present, with the proviso that they had two hours to spend it.)

You can show you care about the personal and professional development of people by sending them to courses and events, or even just on an outing for general inspiration. I've been known to grab our design team and take them out for impromptu trips around the city, from bookstores to cafés to craft stores.

You can reinforce the value of people's input by having an open ear and regular team vision sessions (we can often be seen in the park, with sketchbooks in hand). You can promote wellness by encouraging midday workouts, by organizing weekly exercise sessions (we have yoga on our deck every Friday), or through super simple initiatives, such as buying a blender and encouraging people to share a smoothie each morning.

Part of developing culture is also about the intangible benefits you create. For instance, you can offer flexibility in return for going the extra mile when a deadline looms or a big project is under way. You can instill trust and loyalty by letting people work offsite or at home at key times.

And finally, you must create a space to match. In my experience, an extraordinary culture equals extraordinary output. When people love the space in which they work, they'll want to be there, they'll be inspired to be there, and they'll care deeply about being there.

When my book publishing business took off, I had to throw staff at it immediately, but we were in a tiny, shared office space. So all of a sudden, I had seven staffers and just two phones, and everyone was sitting around one five-seater dining room table. We were hemmed in by boxes of books and had phone and computer cords crisscrossing the office in every direction.

When the phone rang, someone would answer it, put the person on hold (read: hand over the mouthpiece), and pass the phone across the table to whoever was required. It was chaotic, disorganized, and not conducive to an efficient or creative environment in the slightest.

And to make matters worse, there were two other companies on either side of us, playing competing music—and one person was continuously nagging us because we weren't putting the communal cutlery back in the drawer properly. It was definitely time to move out.

Part of my approach with culture is to create an office that feels like a home. If you want to be a family, you need a home, right?

If your culture is your brand, then you need to create a space to match. I have always been happy to invest time and money into creating a gorgeous office space, knowing that an inspiring and nurturing space will in return inspire and nurture those within it.

Sounds simple? It is, but it can make a world of difference. I'm anti-beige, anti-suits, anti–uncomfortable chairs, and anti–boring old boardrooms. I'm for a stocked fridge, a comfy couch, a yoga-occupied deck, an onsite shower, loads of natural light, air, plants, kids, and animals and whatever else is needed to help your staff lead the working life they want.

Our company culture and our people are what we make them. They're worth the investment—for them and for us.

INVEST
in your
PEOPLE

BE FLEXIBLE

Let
opportunity
RUN FREE

Your
CULTURE
is Your
BRAND
it's your
MESSAGE
to the WORLD

INVEST
IN YOU

Your real estate portfolio, your products on the shelf, your cash reserves, even your best staff—it's easy to think that these are by far your best assets. You wouldn't be far wrong.

But I have also always been a big believer in the power of the bits you can't see. Intellectual property is a given, but that's a topic for another day. I'm talking about . . . you!

I'm talking about the mind that buzzes at four a.m. with new ideas, and the people you think and theorize with to make incredible things happen. It is our minds, our education, and our networks that need just as much love and protection as anything else.

After all, one crazy thought in the night—which is well-nurtured, thanks to the seminar you attended, the connection you just made, or the consultant you've recently hired—can be executed and strategically distributed through your networks, and before you know it, voilà, the rest can be history.

Neglect any of these pillars and you'll pay the price. It can happen all too easily. You get too busy or too stressed to let your mind wander and theorize. You ignore the calendar reminder to listen to that mind-blowing podcast while you jog. Or the clincher: You feel you're too busy to get to those midweek mingling events or that out-of-town conference, which is so costly and time-consuming.

What usually happens (I've seen it and I've been there) is that it results in your getting stuck in the same old, same old. You're not breaking through the clutter or standing out from the crowd, resulting in no new wins, no office dance parties or moments of fist-pumping joy and achievement.

And these moments? They are pure oxygen for an entrepreneur. Starve yourself of these opportunities to shine and you'll slowly wither and, as sad as it sounds, die. Okay, maybe that's a bit dramatic, but I do take this very seriously. Continuous self-improvement and incessant investment in you, the entrepreneur, is what will propel you forward.

I remember one of the first times this came into play for me personally. It quite literally changed my life. But each time didn't come without a cost. I'm not talking about fluffy costs like time or in-kind resources. I'm talking about cold, hard cash when, during the early stages of my business, every dollar counted.

About a decade ago, everyone seemed to be talking about this one particular guy. I looked into him and found that he was about to have a two-day conference, but the ticket price was $1,200. This at the time seemed ridiculously out of my reach (which is why I used the word *but*, not *and*—I have since learned this is an important distinction).

I labored on and eventually thought, *Stuff it, I need this.* On the cusp of expanding my thinking—it was time to think big—I bit the bullet and booked my place at his event. I don't think I even had any real publishing clients at the time, so I had no real income to speak of. Against that backdrop, the $1,200 price tag was about $1,199 too much.

But thank goodness for that $1,200 check (and no, it didn't bounce). I learned hundreds of things, really meaty ideas that I could take home straightaway and implement. The conference also threw me into a room with smart, innovative people. It lifted me. It challenged me.

And during the breaks, I met at least three people who within a week I signed up for projects worth between $40,000 and $60,000 each. If we say an average $50,000 for each client, that's a 12,400 percent return on investment. And just like that, this iteration of my career took off. That event connected me with many new clients and their networks, and for that, I'll forever be indebted.

The second break was personal. It was around the same time and I had some issues that needed to be resolved. I knew it, I just didn't know how. Consulting for a recruitment company, I overheard an office conversation about a woman who had done the Hoffman Process and how it had changed her life. I soon learned that the course would cost $5,000 and eight days of my time. This was well before the days of the $1,200 conference, so I was even more broke (both in cash and spirituality at the time). I raised the $500 deposit (I'm still not exactly sure how) and prayed that the rest would come.

Fast-forward to day one of the retreat: It's not even lunchtime and I am already thinking that I would have paid $20,000 for the experience—and I had seven and a half days to go. That course completely and utterly changed my life forever. It woke me up and gave me a true idea of who I am, what my values are, and what I want from life.

I'm a big believer in getting out there and making your life—

and your success—happen. I still balk and whine about spending money on occasion, but when the opportunities come knocking, I think, *C'mon, Lisa, you're playing a bigger game now. Step up. Be brave. Be seen. Get out there.* And then I think, *It's an investment, and you just need one contact, one big idea, one wow moment and that money will come flooding back a hundredfold.*

It's a practice I've continued to this day. I'm never afraid to spend money on things that I feel will positively impact the business or me. In the magazine's first six months, I flew to Rome for the FIPP World Congress, the largest magazine media event in the world. When I arrived, I discovered that few independent titles did this.

It was amazing on so many levels, but one key serendipitous moment springs to mind. On the first night I was fortunate enough to sit next to the vice president and international editorial director of Martha Stewart Living Omnimedia. A week later, I was in Martha's offices chatting about how we could feature one of the world's most incredible entrepreneurs in the magazine. She was the cover girl on our one-year anniversary issue.

It took money and time to go to that conference, but it was the conduit for meeting a series of incredible people to help take the magazine to the next level. All of that for a few thousand dollars. Absolutely priceless for me and the business.

We must continually check in with ourselves. Knowledge and mind-sets are powerful assets. They can mean the difference between living a life of abundance and reciprocity—or not.

Some other personal priorities to consider, which can easily get missed in the hectic schedule of business, include:

YOUR ATTITUDE

An entrepreneur's attitude is the sum total of your values, beliefs, and dreams. It's your perception of yourself and others in the world, the way you treat yourself and others, and the way you think about and approach life. Who are you? If you want to be someone, be yourself.

You must also take personal responsibility for whatever happens in your life, where you have any level of control over the outcome. It's so easy to shift blame onto others. I made my mind up many years ago to look at my side of the street first and always. I cannot change anything that others do or say or the way in which they behave, but I sure as hell can change the way I respond and act. This is a simple (but not always easy) behavioral shift.

YOUR HEALTH

It's often not until you lose something or lose hold of it that you fully appreciate it, and without your health you cannot fire on all cylinders in any area of life. I definitely maintain a health-first mantra, because in my view a healthy body most definitely equals a healthy mind. It's hard to run a business or be a good friend, family member, leader, partner, or lover when your health is compromised. People often comment on my abundance of energy, asking where I get it all from. I am grateful for the health that I have, but I also don't take it for granted, and even when things get tough in the office, I make sure I can still get out there and look after my body.

My non-negotiables are three to four training sessions a week (these are high-energy, fully charged sessions where I push my-self to my physical limits, but it's funny how in these moments I often have my best ideas). At the very least, it's a great release of built-up pressure and frustration. I try to eat well (go, green smoothie) and I make time for myself.

We have a big deck overlooking Sydney city at our office and it's filled with plants; I'm often out there, clippers in hand, chopping away at some greenery. I might be out there for only a few min-utes, but it's enough to have some calm and regroup without all the constancy of noise. And once a week, there's yoga on the deck for the team. I outsource the organization of most of my health activities—mostly because it keeps me accountable, forces me to set goals and have other people championing me to achieve them.

YOUR PERSONAL
AND PROFESSIONAL NETWORKS

There is an old saying that goes something along the lines of "We are the sum of the five people we spend the most time with." I have certainly found this to be true. And we all know that there are some people in our lives who build us up and others who, often unintentionally, drag us down.

In that vein, I always try to surround myself with incredible, inspiring, happy, positive, open, and courageous people. I believe it's important to have a good mix of friends. Some of my friends are insatiable business people, and when we get together, we can bounce around the biggest and most obscure ideas and feed off one another; we almost get high from insane, intellectual conversations.

I have a deep spiritual connection with other friends, and we'll talk philosophy into the early hours of the morning. Other friends are just the funniest people on the planet and we'll talk crazy stories (often involving bad toilet humor) and laugh for hours. On some level every single one of them makes me be the very best version of me. And that is insanely healthy and essential.

We must ensure that those around us, at the end of the day, will help us be the best version of ourselves. Your life partner is all of these things in some way; mine certainly is. He just gets me. I know unequivocally that I'm the best version of me when he is around, and I'm truly grateful for that. Be brave and courageous. If there are people in your life who belittle you, depress you, negatively challenge you, or encourage the worst sides of you, think about getting out of those relationships or, at the very least, reducing the amount of time you spend with them.

YOUR TIME

The more successful in business you become, the more interested and intrigued others will be. This is a wonderful, beautiful thing. I almost fell over the first time someone asked me to sign an autograph for them. One of my staff turned to me as they walked off and joked, "You'll need a minder soon!" But on a serious level, you will have to be careful about how you structure your time.

I absolutely love meeting with people, sharing ideas, and inspiring one another on whatever journeys we are on, but I have had to get smarter with my time and realize that for now I simply cannot meet with everyone, answer every email (that pains me), or attend every function or event. It's as much about protecting your health (physical and mental) as anything else, by ensuring that you put some boundaries in place in this area.

Realize that you won't be able to have coffee with everyone. Conversely, when you have coffee with those further down the business road than you, be grateful for their time and investment in you, but try to give back to them energetically. Don't just take what you can and run. It comes back to my approach that everything should be a mutually beneficial partnership, whether we're talking about money or simply the exchange of ideas and philosophies. We should see ourselves as equals with one another and expect—and offer—a fair exchange in every situation.

YOUR PERSONAL BRAND

I've always been cognizant of the power of your personal brand—and how, if it is harnessed correctly, it can help you stand out from the crowd, leapfrog competitors, break through the clutter, and have a massive impact on the world at large.

How you present yourself at every single touch point should be seamless and consistent. It should be authentic, cohesive, dependable, and genuine. It should reflect who you are, how you want to be seen, and who you want to be in the world. When people talk with you over email, on the phone, or in person, or when they see you in the media, on your website, or at a speaking gig, then your aesthetic—how you speak and what you say—should be consistent. It should also be real. In every single connection point with others.

So you need to get very clear about how you want to be perceived and what message you want to give to the world, whether you are the face of your business or are working within a larger corporation with an existing external brand (remembering that your personal brand is still crucial in that environment). You need to think carefully: What do you want to be known for? How do you want people to think about you? What is your point of difference? If all the "best practice" things are already a given, how will you stand out from the crowd? Get clear on this and then amplify it.

These days more than ever, we live in a fast-paced media world where everyone is a brand, whether they like it or not. Times have certainly changed from when I started in business, when you could just rely on the goodwill of PR in print media or on radio or TV to build your reputation. Blogs, social media platforms, and instant news sources have fast-tracked things and now allow people to easily create a presence and a reputation much, much more easily than in the past. But it takes care, skill, and attention to create the type of authentic brand that people trust and want to connect with on an ongoing basis.

And most important, be consistent. Don't get trapped in something you can't maintain. Ask yourself what you want your personal brand to be (if you haven't determined it already) by examining yourself: Who am I, what do I stand for, and what am I going to tell the world about?

In the early stages of business, you might think it's ridiculous to even consider such things, but if you find success even on a smaller scale (let's hope it's gigantic!), then your public brand will have a role to play. If you have found success, ask yourself if you're still on brand or if some tweaks need to take place.

A FEW QUICK
and very practical
BRAND TIPS

SECURE ALL YOUR NAMES AS FAST AS YOU CAN.

Domain names, Twitter handles, Instagram, Facebook, Snapchat, and the like for yourself and your business. (I even have friends who have done this for their toddler, just in case they want them later on in life.) There's nothing worse than having to rely on lawyers to get a name back, or worse, not to be able to get it back at all (been there, done that). So learn from me—get a jump on it and save yourself the time, hassle, and money.

CONNECTIONS ARE KING.

Ensure you are connected to everyone you know using all of the online platforms at your disposal. Brand awareness is more than just the old adage about "it's who you know." It's also not just who you know, but what they know about you. It's what they know of your personal brand and how they perceive you, and what your reputation is. Communicate with people openly and constantly. Network avidly. Let people develop a strong relationship with you.

PURPOSEFULLY MIX WITH THE RIGHT PEOPLE.

Be found among the movers and shakers, the influencers, the people who will help you foster, grow, and champion your brand. Again, though, think value exchange, because there is nothing worse than a one-way relationship (business or otherwise).

GET CLEAR ON WHAT YOU WANT TO BE KNOWN FOR.

Know your core values, your belief system, who you are, and what you stand for. When people think X, do they think you? You want to be the go-to person for the brand you create. Keep reinventing and reinvigorating yourself, staying fresh and relevant.

THINK ABOUT WHAT LEGACY YOU WANT TO CREATE.

As part of the multilayered personal development I have done over the years, one cathartic exercise had me lying next to a gravestone in a cemetery (I kid you not) for several hours, imagining that I was dead in the ground. Actually you can do this right now. (You don't have to find a cemetery to do this, but it does deepen the experience.) Imagine your funeral. Who is there? What are they saying about you? Now step back to the present day and make the necessary changes to make your days, months, and years count in the way you want them to. This is just as much a part of your brand as it is a part of you.

BECOME THE BEST.

Keep learning, educating yourself, updating your knowledge, and challenging yourself. You need to become the expert in whatever it is you have chosen, because if you are going to pump your brand out there, you want to be damn sure that you can back it up. Develop a highly identifiable personality. What makes people think of you? What are the characteristics and skills that make you unique and memorable? What will make people connect with you and feel confident in the services you offer or the products you sell?

CREATE CHANGE.

You need to be an active force in your field. You need to be ahead of the pack and constantly innovating and making a significant contribution to your industry/ies.

STiMULATE
YOUR MIND
Educate Your
BRAIN
Explore
LEAVE
the office
VALUE
your
TIME

GIVE yourself a BREAK TRAVEL respect your HEALTH challenge your thinking

LEVERAGE
IT ALL

I've always been a deal broker. It's one of my favorite things to do, almost more than anything else. I just love connecting people and I love creating and facilitating value exchange. I don't use those words lightly or by accident. They are used with extreme purpose because they seem to represent a concept that people have the most difficulty coming to terms with.

Before I started my first company in 2001, I worked for a sponsorship agency where my entire job was to broker deals. I had a great deal of respect for my boss at the time, but I remember vividly that I had him constantly rolling his eyes as I kept banging on and on about strategic alliances and non-monetary deals. It drove him nuts because as far as he was concerned, there was only one currency in an exchange, and that was money.

I'm proud to say that back in that job, I did do countless monetary deals. The truth is, regardless of what job, industry, or market you are in, we all need to be able to build relationships and ultimately sell stuff.

But I also negotiated plenty of exchanges where money wasn't the only currency, because I'm a massive believer in finding like-minded, noncompeting partners who share similar customer bases and can leverage from one another. More often than not, these were the deals that left every party feeling like a winner. You

DJ at my event and I'll do the PR for your book. You subsidize the catering for our conference and we can arrange a series of business consulting sessions to help with your newly appointed team. You promote me to your 200,000-strong database and I'll record a series of six how-to videos specifically tailored to your market. You promote my tour on your product, and on my tour I'll give away samples of your product. I'll give you 500 copies of my book to sell to your audience and I'll become a regular contributor to your entire database. I design and attach my brand to you for a clothing collaboration in exchange for a fee and/or profit and exposure in your 150 stories globally.

It can be as small as you like right through to the massive, like one of my favorite campaigns and collaborations of all time, the one between Jay-Z and Bing, where fans were asked to unearth more than 300 pages of his soon-to-be-released autobiography in 600 unique advertising placements in fifteen cities across the world and in Bing Maps. The global treasure hunt was incredible, with pages of his book lining the bottom of a swimming pool and hiding on a building's rooftop, resulting in trans-media storytelling and insane media interest with one billion impressions. The market share of Bing—who wanted to increase their relevance with Gen Y and to create engagement with their new mapping software—hit its highest percentage since its launch. Absolute integrative-thinking brilliance.

The brand partnership between James Cameron's award-winning movie *Avatar* and Coca-Cola Zero upon the film's release was said to have rewritten the rules of brand partnerships, mostly because there was no monetary transaction. Instead, both parties saw the alliance as a complete value exchange. In short, Coca-Cola Zero used augmented reality technology so their drinkers could interact with 3-D motion graphics from the film. They branded cans as well as cinema cups. There was also a TV commercial and cinema spot created by Coca-Cola Zero and Twentieth Century Fox in which a young man who was drinking a can of *Avatar*-branded Coca-Cola Zero at his computer was suddenly transported to Pandora. Coca-Cola's Joe Tripodi said that for them, the value was connecting in a more relevant way with a target audience, which in that case was young men aged eighteen to thirty-four who were into gaming and science fiction.

I can understand that to some people, these sorts of partnerships can seem so out of the box and so difficult to arrange that they can be intimidating. In fact, when I start to talk like this (read: ramble enthusiastically, gaining gusto with every phrase) about sponsorships and strategic partners, people look at me like I have two heads.

But in my view, negotiating mutually beneficial value exchanges is at the core of every successful enterprise. In my many years in business, I've structured deals across the globe in almost every conceivable way. You name a way; I've probably structured it.

That is because businesses that really amplify and scale know how to do partnerships and do them well. It is often more necessity than anything else that forces entrepreneurs to think creatively and laterally early on, as budding businesses don't generally have a lot of resources to throw at partnerships.

They frequently have less to offer than their competitors—fewer people, less money, and less of a track record in the marketplace. As a result, they simply must do more with less. But the positive they bring to the table is that they are fast, nimble, flexible, and lean and are not tied into existing systems and bureaucracy, so they can mold themselves and their products into mutually beneficial partnerships much more easily. It means they are able to play in the same field, but a different game.

With millions of dollars behind them, big businesses can push their messaging out and reach all the marketplace. A start-up can't. But you still need to find ways to attract customers, and partnerships can be a great way to do this. It means that at times you need to become a master of leverage, which is simply the art of doing more with less.

I once asked a client who their target market was. They said doctors, so I asked how they were going to get to doctors. Their strategy was to individually call and mail every single doctor in Australia. I was shocked! "Why would you do that?" I asked. Why not go to the overarching bodies that have preexisting relationships with all the doctors, offer them something attractive, and get them to do the sell for you? Rather than have tens of thousands of touch points, you would have just one. They did, and they succeeded; this was all about the power of leverage.

If you're not exchanging money, then what are you exchanging and how do you do it? It might be brand alignment, media opportunities, exposure, access to customers, access to data, access to already prospected customers in specific target markets, in-kind support, the opportunity to cobrand a product, purchase a product, or sell one, and so forth.

When brokering partnerships, you can't see yourself as a smaller version of a big business. You must think of yourself as a completely new, innovative entity that happens to be playing in the same industry. By thinking this way, you will see yourself as a valuable proposition, as opposed to a small player begging for money or non-monetary support.

You have something to offer them just as much as they have something to offer you. As a result, how you market yourself needs to be massively different from how the existing players are doing it, if you are going to forge partnerships.

When it comes to the negotiation, don't make it all about you. Not once have I ever pitched to another party by talking all about my product or me. Instead, I focus on explaining how we both can benefit from the situation, with greater emphasis on them and their goals than on me and mine. (And only ever after the initial meeting, having taken a brief.) The PowerPoint thing has almost become a running joke over the years. When some of our big distribution partners or other people ask my marketing director before we go into a big pitch "What are you taking?" she simply says, "Lisa." I am the material.

You don't necessarily need PowerPoint presentations or visual aids to help get a deal over the line; we rarely use them because I think that people end up talking to the presentation rather than to the people in the room. You often end up using them as a crutch; worse, they can be an instant killer of authenticity, connection, and passion.

What you do need is to know your subject matter so well that you can quickly think on your feet and structure a deal about any intricacy of your subject, once the other party's wishes are laid out on the table.

Here is a little tip. I believe that almost every person working for a corporation secretly yearns to be an entrepreneur. And so, given half the chance to somehow be a part of a fun, entrepreneurial project that takes them beyond their day job and gives them a taste of an entrepreneur's crazy life, they will commit, if you can give them some commercial justification.

There are a zillion different types of deals to be done and ways to procure investment and support for your venture. You can pitch for seed funding, angel funding, support from venture capitalists, and so forth. Then of course there is crowdfunding, which has become increasingly popular in the past couple of years; we have forward-thinking organizations like Kickstarter and GoFundMe to thank for that. And then there are corporate deals, which is the space I have the most experience in.

The first thing you need to focus on as an entrepreneur is what's in it for them. It's not about having structured sponsorship deals (even if you have ten—most people have only three, the tried and true gold, silver, and bronze), as they are just too rigid for today's corporations and the ultra-specific, measurable, leveraged outcomes they seek.

Before I worked in sponsorship (my job prior to starting my first business), I worked in conference and event management, where everyone used to sell gold, silver, and bronze cookie-cutter sponsorship packages that included branding, ticketing/hospitality, and little else.

And then they would wonder why sponsors would never return the following year.

There were no bespoke benefits, no relationships fostered, and no leveraging of the partnership over a period of time beyond that one event. In essence, there was no real distinguishable value in exchange for the cold hard cash that these corporates were forking out. The deal was signed, and then the sponsor was forgotten about.

I saw it time and time again, and I knew that there had to be a different, more engaging, and simply smarter way to do business. It was then that I decided to conduct these deals as if these people were my friends, as if we were in a real relationship and I cared about their success from this arrangement.

It changed the way I viewed the transaction. It became a genuine value exchange, as I wanted to find a way that we could help each other be successful, forming relationships and exchanges that would be mutually beneficial and symbiotic by nature. As a result, I hoped that we would want to continue working together over and over again.

I decided that I would truly look at what their objectives were, and they would look at mine, so that we could work together toward achieving these goals. That's when it became fun for me, because it didn't become about what currency was being exchanged. It became all about the outcome. It excites me just writing about it.

This notion is how I run my business every single day and forms the basis for all my relationships and deals. Is there a fair and equitable exchange? This is the same for business and life and is very different from thinking, *I need to get something from everything.*

When I came to this realization, everything changed and doing deals became easy. How easy is it when you find companies you feel you have a good fit with, who are aligned with your values, vision, and audience, and with whom you can genuinely find a way to help one another? Sometimes (depending on the size of the "property" or assets you are offering), the exchange will be money coming your way; other times it will be everything but money. And that is not necessarily a bad thing.

Deals can be about money, but they can also be about brand recognition. Early on, I brokered a deal between a prominent children's entertainment group and a margarine company. The deal was simple: The margarine company could include a picture of the entertainers on a couple of million tubs of margarine a week, in the hope that kids shopping with their mums would encourage a sale. The margarine company paid handsomely for the privilege, as they knew it would help them to sell more margarine.

Well, that was a good deal, I thought, so now, having a great relationship with the brand manager at the margarine company at the time, I asked him who else sat within their brand stable, and he suggested a baking conglomerate who might want the same group on their loaves of bread. Another deal was done.

By now relationships were ticking along and all the parties involved were excited, so I decided to layer it up a bit more. Bread and butter were selling like hotcakes and the entertainment group had its face all over Australia, which is exactly what they wanted. But their current tour was ending and I thought, *I need to get one more deal in before my window of opportunity closes.*

I suggested a competition in which kids could vie for the entertainers to play in their home. We rolled out a simple on-pack promotion—more product sales, more group amplification, and on it went. Everyone was winning.

Deals can also be about incentivizing customers. A deal I did in the early 2000s comes to mind, when I was selling sponsorship for a motivational speaker, huge in the entrepreneurial space at the time.

It was (in the beginning) a standard tiered sponsorship approach, but then I met with a stockbrokerage company that wanted to attract people to their services. Rather than having them just pay a wad of cash to be listed as a sponsor and arranging to get their logo on everything, I negotiated a deal of a sort that to my knowledge hadn't really ever been done.

We put in place a mechanism to incentivize the audience to join the brokerage website, and once they had joined, we would track and measure their activity. Payment from the sponsor to the speaker's tour would occur only if the customer used the broker's product.

The tour management took a lot of convincing. They thought it was too much of a risk on their part. As it turned out, we all pulled off quite a coup. It was one of the first big deals I had done and netted approximately three times what the stockbrokerage would have otherwise paid.

Within my book business, I presold titles in the thousands to corporations and organizations who were looking for a product to align with, or who simply wanted a quality product they could give away to clients, customers, and staff—something more meaningful than a hat or a branded stress ball. Banks, cosmetic companies, car brands, stationery brands, charities—you name it, we worked with them. For example, a premium car dealer could use a coffee table book to incentivize test drives. A cosmetic brand could use a book on how to apply makeup to incentivize a purchase or reward repeat customers. Real estate agents could present a book on how to decorate your home to buyers as they receive the keys to their new home. You get the gist. The opportunities are endless as long as it's a win-win for both parties involved.

In other cases, we partnered with high-profile business people and CEOs who wanted to appear as experts on the book's topic, and so books were customized with a page or two from the company's CEO.

And everyone walked away happy—we moved books in volume (any author will tell you how amazing that is for the bottom line), enjoyed credibility with a wider audience, and had leverage options, while the corporations obtained customized or highly relevant books without having to produce them from scratch or pay a full recommended retail price (the price was always discounted, based on the quantity purchased).

As for the magazine, its success—and the reason for its rapid global expansion—has been built on a plethora of deals structured in just about every way possible, always with like-minded noncompeting parties. They have been all about brand alignment, synergy in values, and audience profiles. Some have comprised media partnerships, while others are a trade and value exchange of some kind. Whatever the case, the principle remains the same: All parties must walk away from every deal a winner.

We've created a range of different properties within the *Collective Hub*™ brand and have been able to broker hundreds of deals as a result—some big, many small, but all of value to us. It has been about identifying assets across the print magazine and our digital platforms; social media, Web, email, and direct mail campaigns to existing and potential readers; product collaborations; my time as a public speaker; and the list goes on and on. Everything you offer to someone has a monetary value attached to it and is attractive to the right partner. You trade either for money or for leverage of one kind or another, depending on what they have to offer and what is attractive to you or your brand at that point in time. It is a dance of building and valuing equity between both parties. There is a constant ability to trade and there is a constant need for recognition of what you value and where the exchange is.

THINK
OUTSIDE
the BOX
COLLABORATION
is key
THINK
on your
FEET

MONEY
is not the
only CURRENCY
the
POSSIBILITIES
are
LIMITLESS

DISRUPT

Y ou are that person who jumps off a cliff and learns to fly on the way down." This is a phrase I've heard, in one iteration or another, for almost my entire career (even more so since the *Collective Hub™* began).

I am. Proudly. In saying that, this willingness to jump first and think later shouldn't be confused with recklessness. There's a lot of careful planning and strategy involved, because it's ultimately all about taking calculated risks.

If you were to ask my mum, she'd probably say that I was born a disrupter. That's probably a polite way of saying I was rebellious, argumentative, rowdy, and interrogative, although I like to think she means I was curious, free-spirited, and expressive! I was such a handful that she shipped me off to boarding school when I was fourteen years old, even though we lived just a mile or so away; she endured the extra cost despite not really being able to afford it because she couldn't handle my "leap first, think later" attitude, which incidentally I've had my whole life.

My grandfather, a highly intelligent and politically focused leader, would often suggest that he could "throw a bucket of cold water" over me to tone me down. But because he had a glint of pride and amusement in his eyes when he said this, I knew that he secretly loved my spirit. Indeed, after I grew up, he would entertain my zany ideas for hours at a time. He was my rock and always believed in me. I miss him every day but feel his guiding presence with me continuously.

When I was fifteen or so, I had guitar lessons at school, but I don't remember my fingers ever hitting the strings. That's because I spent most of the time on the carpeted green steps outside the classroom in forced exile. I was always in trouble because I relentlessly challenged the status quo.

In math class one day, the teacher came over and without a word picked my chair and me up and carried us both outside; he plonked me down on the ground and walked back inside, closing the door behind him. His frustration at my incessant questioning of absolutely everything he said had clearly reached the boiling point.

Later, when I was an employee, bosses strong and secure enough to endure questioning and a steady flow of new ideas and suggestions loved me. They championed my abilities, and in every job I held, I moved through the ranks very quickly (often to the annoyance of my fellow employees).

I always wanted equity in every company I ever worked for— looking back, I was a bit of a brat—although I barely had any real understanding of what that even meant at the time.

I'm a little savvier now, but otherwise I haven't changed. I still behave just like that in business, although perhaps what has changed is that the desire to do things differently or better has greater perspective and a good dose of maturity attached to it.

At school, you have to abide by certain rules, and the same is true if you are working in a corporation, so it's no wonder I was never going to last too long in either area.

I find it rather ironic now when people from my past champion me as a rebel. What kept me in constant trouble back in the day now perpetually holds me in good stead. Throughout my formal education, I was always in conflict with the powers that be because of my independent attitude and persistence in questioning the status quo, but now I get asked to go back and speak at my school about my success. I was even made alumnus of the year by my university. The whole notion of this really fascinates me.

Looking back on boarding school, I am grateful for some parts—mostly that my mother scrimped and saved to get me there, even though she didn't have the money to afford it—but I still feel like the educational system remains far behind in fostering the entrepreneurial spirit.

Something seems very out of whack there. One of my greatest yearnings is to infiltrate the educational system with positivity and choice so that future graduating classes can avoid years of soul-searching, mistakes, and therapy later in life. It is my confidence, emotional intelligence, and maturity that have changed and now I have more authority to influence others.

I ended up going to university, but only because it was expected that I would do so, and I studied tourism, of all things (okay, it was a business degree, but I majored in tourism). I excelled in my law and communications subjects and won the school's alumnus award—and then the overall alumnus of the year—out of a potential pool of over 40,000.

Back at boarding school, my best friend, Kerry, and I were always in weekend and evening detention. My first week there, I was grounded on the school property for six weeks because chocolate was found in my room, and having any food in your room was strictly contraband. As a result, I missed what would have been my first ever U2 concert. I was devastated.

Another time, we dyed our hair purple with what turned out to be a permanent color. Grounded for another six weeks.

One Saturday, we were in detention again and found ourselves philosophizing about the entire situation. Even though the whole institution truly pissed us off, we surmised that surely the teachers and administrators were adults and they must know what they were doing. We've continued to talk about it a lot as adults and we still think they had no idea.

Society tries to constrain us—it wants us to fit into the status quo and just do as we are asked, buy the things we are told to and do the things expected of us—but we don't have to be constrained. People let themselves be dictated to and stifled, but you can question, think, and push the boundaries if you want to in a smart, respectful way.

I was disruptive throughout my formal education (notice how that's usually deemed a negative?), and I continue to disrupt in my career. You can disrupt in business as an individual by having an insatiable desire for new ideas and an understanding of the architecture required to build the systems and processes to implement them.

Disrupters are successful because they are not afraid of

change. They are not so embedded in an industry that they can see only one way of doing things. They are forward-thinking and open-minded and often start moving well before they fully understand the market they're entering or trying to change.

When you've been in an industry for a while, it's easy to think you know it all, have seen it all, and have tried it all. Disrupters disagree. There's always another way, another approach, something untried that might just work.

As a business owner, I find that there is nothing better than entering an age-old industry, flipping it on its head, and doing something totally counterintuitive to what is expected. This is where most entrepreneurs thrive: looking at industries that are stuffy, struggling, conservative, or old-hat and throwing a dose of business mojo their way. I am not criticizing the individuals within any industries I have entered, but rather, the scale and therefore rigidity of some of the businesses and processes within them.

Kickstarter is just one example of this. Co-founder Perry Chen wanted to bring a pair of DJs to play at a jazz concert, but didn't have the spare cash floating around to fund it. Frustrated that the audience had no say in the matter, he created a new way for people to raise money, ushering in the concept of crowdfunding to an unsuspecting—but very grateful—world. And the traditional funding world is still trying to catch up.

In a similar vein, live streaming sites like Spotify and Pandora have sent the music industry into a spin and forced a metamorphosis to ensure it would survive the digital era (that's still a work in progress). And then there's Uber, the billion-dollar enterprise that freaked out entire taxi systems across the world, and Airbnb, which suggested a new way for people to travel.

Disrupters take an idea and run wildly with it, often launching into a market of unsuspecting, sleepy competitors. This gives the disrupter a distinct advantage, because the existing players are often suspicious of their approach, slow to react, and certain they will fail. Until they don't.

These disrupters are the dreamers, the risk-takers, those inspired by innovation and unafraid of failure. They are willing to examine an existing industry and propose a new landscape. They are nimble enough to move when others can't and are courageous enough to keep going when others would bail.

They are, as Richard Branson says, the ones who "passionately believe it is possible to change the industry, to turn it on its head, to make sure that it will never be the same again."

The author and motivational speaker Jason Jennings published a book called *It's Not the Big That Eat the Small . . . It's the Fast That Eat the Slow*. I am a massive believer in this philosophy. If you ever use size, lack of industry knowledge, or lack of money as an excuse, I'm going to call you on your BS! What you're really saying is that you are simply not passionate and determined enough. You are not a born disrupter. So either move on or eat a bucket of cement for breakfast, grow some cojones, and step up.

To disrupt takes a lot of guts, self-belief, tenacity, and determination. I'm not going to lie to you: This game is not for the weak or the faint of heart.

When I launched the *Collective Hub™*, I entered an age-old industry with no magazine experience behind me—much the same as I did with books really, just on a much bigger, riskier, crazier scale. I don't think people actually believe me, so let's get really clear on it: I had never worked for or on a magazine. Most of my staff at the time had never worked for or on a magazine.

I was entering an industry that was being heralded from the rooftops as a dying one; print magazines were biting the dust all over the place. Barriers and cost of entry were massive, and I was doing this entirely on my own with no financial backers.

Distribution channels were multilayered and complex. I've since learned just how complex it is: The magazine now has literally hundreds of distribution partnerships in Australia alone, and it is just one of the dozens of countries we are currently in.

And I was coming at it saying I wasn't going to rely on advertising dollars. Traditionally, magazine revenue streams are comprised of primarily advertising, newsstand sales, and subscriptions. Advertising is often the biggest slice of the pie. But I relied on my past experience, brought lessons from other industries, and tried different revenue streams like preselling to corporations or coming up with multifaceted partnerships that brought together a range of salable units, where the magazine was just one component.

We then launched into eleven countries immediately, instead of starting out small and slow. I wanted to be global from the outset. What's more, we launched without telling anyone in the traditional media industry or making any public statements. There wasn't a hint of PR that this little baby was on its way.

And that was it: disruption done.

Now all we needed to do was keep it going! Looking back at my personal journal from that time, this is what I wrote one evening during those chaotic early days:

What a crazy rollercoaster of a ride the the start-up life is —
today feels like **Christmas**

BUTTERFLIES in my stomach

excited, my brain buzzing constantly
people believe in us like I have never
witnessed ~~??~~ TEARS OF JOY.
Dropped to my knees
Digging deep for self-belief
so on purpose, JUGGLING
Balls in the air,   first cover shot
someone gave me a picture saying
"the CHOSEN one

so many sentimental moments like this.

Exclusive deal with MUMBRELLA to
freak the story. TALK of the TOWN.

Energy is palpable. - HAPPY DANCE -
Such a beautiful sense of community

EXTRAORDINARY!   'bigger than me, bubble
of love, good feelings,
selling its socks off.

Finally, we've nailed it!

Our approach with books was also quite disruptive. Most people who write books lack funding and distribution, but I saw a group in the market (mostly motivational speakers or those who had access to a reader market) who had both: the means to pay for the publishing of a book and the ability to move sales once the book arrived, essentially removing the need for a publishing house.

And they wanted speed to market, which most traditional publishing houses could not offer—traditional publishers plan twelve to eighteen months in advance, but we were turning books around in just a few months. There are many more ways to broker book publishing deals now, and the industry is much more innovative than it once was, but at the time of starting my book publishing business, there wasn't a lot of flexibility.

By working with us, our clients could walk away with almost all of the profits instead of the 10 to 15 percent a publishing house normally offers. It also meant they could sell the books direct to their already assembled followers, instead of relying on the convoluted distribution processes of bookstores. We helped our clients get that esteemed bookshop presence as well, just so all bases were covered, and we also suggested some other clever sponsorship and presales ideas they could employ to move volume or generate funding early on if required.

By using these unique partnerships and sponsorship strategies, I sold 36,000 copies of my first book *Happiness Is . . .* in its first year of publication. Just after my book had been released and I was busy soliciting sales deals and multifaceted partnerships, a company I had been chatting with called and said, "We've just sent you a purchase order for eight thousand copies of your book. Could you have them here within five weeks?"

Holding my composure, I said it would be arranged as requested before getting off the phone and shouting and dancing like a complete idiot. At that time, a bestseller in Australia was 5,000 books and we'd just smashed that out of the park in a one-minute phone call. We'd disrupted . . . and it was working.

So how do you disrupt? The first step is to look at where the gap is. As is the case with most entrepreneurs, your idea was probably born out of frustration—no decent café around here, so I'll start my own; no skin-care products that blend perfectly with my skin, so I'll create my own; no beach umbrella that actually stays in the ground at the beach, so I'll design one that will; and so on.

Then, think about opportunities to address it. Put yourself in the shoes of the consumer and ask yourself, "What would I want from this product or service?" This is where you need to take the lid off the box and go crazy with creativity. You're trying to disrupt, not get along, so turn every concept upside down until the perfect idea strikes.

Think about the Uber guys. They provide mechanisms for pricing to surge with supply and demand: at certain times on New Year's Eve, Uber drivers can charge more to passengers than they would on a random Tuesday morning in May.

They disrupted the traditional taxi mode, and although there are challenges to their model—certain regions, Australia included, want to see their program become more regulated, for reasons of safety and competition—the business continues to thrive. Case in point: In its last funding round, Uber raised $1.2 billion in capital to move forward.

So once you have your disruptive idea, you can map it out from there. Use your business smarts and pull in any helpers that you might need along the way (after all, no one is an island) to deliver your product to the market. You simply need to place one foot in front of the other, handling the challenges as they arise, detouring when you encounter a roadblock, regrouping after bad days, and forging ahead on the good ones, all the while researching the industry you now find yourself in, looking at what it's doing right and what it's potentially doing wrong.

Now, the difference between a start-up and a disruptive start-up is this: start-ups often play it safe and follow the blueprint of what companies before them in that same industry have been doing. They try to emulate it, but make it better.

Disrupters often enter an industry and choose not to look at the existing blueprint, but rather look outside that industry and bring best practice from other industries and apply it in a new, fresh, and different way to the industry in question. Essentially, they attempt to rewrite the rules.

For me, that's the trick—look at the market need, think about the next logical step, and then apply it, all the while drawing on knowledge and lessons learned in other unrelated industries.

One of the reasons disrupters succeed is that they're willing to start before they have all of the information at hand and they're happy to learn as they go. As long as you have business smarts, industry-specific naiveté can be great because you don't know what "can't be done" and you are not constrained by industry norms.

The reality is that for most of the industries I have entered, I have genuinely known little about them at the start but I knew the business skills I did have easily crossed industries.

Also remember, speed is on your side. More established industries can rarely move at the speed of a start-up—especially a disruptive one that has a bomb under it—largely because of their established infrastructure, rules, and bureaucracy that weigh them down like an anchor or at the very least force them to walk as if they're wading through mud.

They may have a board to appease or shareholders to consider or be stuck with a funding model that doesn't allow for a quick change of direction or a reconnaissance mission. And the competition is awesome. Never be afraid of it. You might not have the most money (far from it) or the biggest team, systems, and processes, but if you can move fast, look for the gaps, collaborate with like-minded noncompeting partners, and do things differently, you can actually get ahead of the big players, and fast.

A market loves a rebellious underdog who stuns everyone in sight and provides it with something they all want.

Remember that as a disrupter, you'll almost always live in a state of creation or change because in the early stages of a business everything is always in a perpetual state of flux.

It's hard work for unseasoned punters walking into it and can often look more like chaos and a frenetic mess than a plausible business. That's because you are building everything. You're often entering uncharted territory with no map, blueprint, or rules. It's like the Wild West.

A key problem is throwing new staff at the task, hoping that they will fit. I discussed this at length in the chapter entitled "Culture Up," because getting the culture mix right will have a huge impact on the success of your business. Your employees' roles can consist of two hundred different tasks, and more often than not, job descriptions come with the caveat that they'll need to sink or swim. At that point in the life of the enterprise, there is no process or system to tell them what to do, so they'll have to create it or simply refine whatever might be there.

To some people, particularly those who have spent a lot of time in the corporate world, this is an unimaginable nightmare of epic proportions—and often they will leave. Or worse, you may have to ask them to leave because they can't adapt to their new environment. It's fast. It's frenetic. It's not for the fainthearted. It changes every single day.

In all start-up iterations of my businesses, I have unfortunately witnessed high staff churn in the first six months. It's uncomfortable for everyone involved. For the most part, these casualties were no one's fault, just a result of a fast-paced, evolving workplace where job roles must change as the start-up does. When the leaders jump, the staff must jump as well.

The real positive here is that for those who can evolve and adapt, there are huge personal opportunities for them. My magazine's art director didn't come to me with the intention of being a designer. She started out as a project manager with strong editorial abilities, but today she heads up our entire art team and is one of the savviest, smartest, and most creative people I know. I hope she never leaves. (And I hope she is reading this.) One of our senior designers started as a junior writer, and don't get me started on our marketing director, who literally walked in off the street as a graduate ten years ago, with the most amazing personality and can-do-anything attitude I'd ever seen.

But back to disrupting. One thing's for sure—every hour of every day, things change and no one day will ever be the same, which is why, when you hit a certain critical mass, you must bring in the smarts to help you systemize, develop processes, and bottle the genius in order to scale.

When I have an idea, I write down everything about it I can possibly muster up; it's a word vomit and covers anything and everything in no particular order. I think about how the market could benefit from something new and how the existing industry could be radically different to make it work.

I act as if money were no problem, as if I had all the funding I needed to succeed, because thinking as if you don't can put a brick wall in front of you before you've even had time to imagine what could be. Money always comes if the idea is strong enough.

Then I look at other industries different to the one I want to disrupt. I go on a hunt for "best practice" ideas that could be applied here. I tinker with revenue models, flesh out who might invest into it, shop the idea around to garner a reaction (if appropriate), and essentially search for one credible yes to get me going.

If you have an idea and feel it has serious disruptive potential, determine a few revenue streams to fund it immediately but also look long-term. Know who will buy this product or service, decide if there is a market big enough, and look at the existing competitors and decide if there's enough room in there for a disrupter like you.

And even if you don't have the idea just yet, question everything. Keep pushing and finding different ways to do things and don't do things because other people expect you to or because it's the way it's always been done. There is a path out there designed just for you.

I hope that everything I do is completely and purposefully counterintuitive to the norm. I hope that I will continue to follow a new path instead of the normal, traditional one.

I hope that I'll continue to look at big, bold existing industries and wonder how I can be part of a disruptive move. I hope I'll continue to have the foresight to see things that don't yet even exist, that are beyond even the imagination of the stalwarts of any particular industry. That I'll stay crazy and hungry enough to keep going. That I'll maintain the confidence to do so.

.BE A
pioneer
QUESTION
RETHINK
REDO
when they zig
you zag

SAY **NO** to the
STATUS QUO

SHAKE
things UP !
WRITE*
your own rules

DO GOOD

In a sun-filled room I sat, a bunch of women in blue tracksuits staring straight back at me. I'd never been to a prison before, and in all honesty, I didn't really know what to expect. It was early on in my business life and I had been asked to speak to inmates at an open day about my career journey. I was excited and hopeful but also nervous and unsure.

Off I went, driving ninety minutes from Sydney to a medium-security correctional center to meet a group of new people who were seemingly looking for a new start. As part of their time behind bars, they were offered a number of courses, including one on business skills, and my role was to inspire them about the possibilities once they were back in the real world.

I shared my story and very practically talked them through the steps to opening and running a business, from stocking the stationery cabinet to structuring mutually beneficial deals. I looked at their faces, some warm and curious, others hard and ambivalent. I had no idea of the impact I had made, but hoped something dropped into those hearts that, given time, would begin to grow.

Afterward, a young woman called Elaine came over and we began to chat. She had two kids, had become involved in drugs through working in a hotel in Sydney, and consequently had found herself behind bars. "Wrong crowd," she said frankly, "but this place is not for me. I have big dreams, big goals. I need to get out and make something of myself for my girls. I am going to start a business just like you."

She was determined not to become institutionalized and get in a revolving door of going out and coming back in, as she had seen happen to so many before her. We chatted for about fifteen minutes and hashed out a quick business plan around her idea (she planned to open a beauty salon), and I gave her some tips and hints. I clearly knew nothing of the challenges faced by anyone in prison, but I knew everyone deserved a second chance and I also knew business, so I stuck to that. Then I moved on and chatted with others.

As I left that place, through the multiple rounds of security, the one-way chats to security staff, and the farewells to the course staff who had arranged my visit, Elaine's youthful yet hardened face stayed with me. She had that glint in her eye—a mix of hope and the desire for someone to believe in her, fueled with a dogged determination from the perils of her life to date—and her words to me as I left rang in my ears: "Lisa, I will do this. One day you will see me and know that I have achieved what I said I would." Shivers raced down my spine in that moment. She didn't cry, but I wanted to.

I have no idea what became of Elaine. I hope she is running a beauty salon now and walking her girls to school each day as she had hoped. I have no idea if she's facing cash-flow or staffing issues as I type! But that twentysomething face and what it represented—the desire to change the course of our lives, to be the best version of ourselves we can be—has stayed with me, challenged me, and inspired me to this very day.

From my first day in business, I made a resolution to help others in the process and decided that if that fateful day did come in which I was making lots of money, then I'd also make a difference with it. Luckily, some way into my first business, I learned that the two did not have to be mutually exclusive and that money does indeed give you a platform from which to give back.

My grandfather was an incredibly kind, giving man who sat on multiple charity boards; he was the president of everything from Arthritis Australia to Barnardos Australia, an organization that helps to stop child abuse.

He led trade missions to the Pacific, Asia, Europe, Africa, and North America; was the inaugural president of the Keep Australia Beautiful organization; and was involved with drug and alcohol rehabilitation. As a result, his influence was deeply ingrained in me.

He had always used his platform to help others, and I wanted to do the same. But even when we have this mandate, it's easy to stray off course or get distracted with the crazily busy life of an entrepreneur. The small-business owner wears many hats (that really should say "almost every hat known to humankind!").

A while ago I watched the American-German political war thriller *Blood Diamond*, and it cut me to the core. A massive jolt. If you're a regular reader of our magazine, you may have read this story already, but it was such an intense moment in my life that I have to share it all over again.

I watched the movie at a friend's place, and as the credits

started to roll, I couldn't engage in post-movie banter. I had to get out of there as fast as I could to process what I had just seen in a Sydney family room thousands of miles away from the diamond regions of Africa. I drove home in tears, feeling frustrated, angry, and powerless.

Once home, I got out of the car, put my sneakers on, and did the only thing I could do in the moment: I ran. In the dark and the rain. Alone. I ran and ran and ran until it hurt.

If you haven't seen *Blood Diamond* (released in 2006), it presents the atrocities of the Western-driven diamond trade and the horrific actions and carnage associated with it. As is the case with anything from Hollywood, no one expects the full or correct story—after all, we like a bit of drama and exaggeration when popcorn is in hand—but you can learn from anything in life, even a Hollywood movie.

The year before, I was waiting for a flight with two friends, about to holiday in Morocco when I bought a copy of the book *Hotel Rwanda* at the airport. It's the story of the hotel manager Paul Rusesabagina and how he saved 1,200 people from sure death during the 1994 Rwandan genocide. We were so taken by his story and again, the inaction of the Western world, that we read the book furiously in tandem, ripping pages out and passing them from hand to hand. In the end, all that was left was a pile of ripped, out-of-order pages and three broken hearts.

For all of Hollywood's sins, you have to throw your hat up to anyone pushing for social change. Both occasions (I later watched the movie version of *Hotel Rwanda* and sobbed for about four hours afterward) kicked me in the guts.

And it was a good kick because when you're in business, life is busy and full and rich and challenging. You can easily slip into focusing solely on your immediate needs—the latest disaster or hurdle to overcome—and legitimately be so entangled in the job at hand that you don't have time to look up or out.

I couldn't stop wondering what I was doing—really doing—to have a positive impact, to help make changes, to help with the serious issues of cruelty, poverty, and social injustice on our planet.

What was I doing to create a happier, safer place and a better world?

These are the moments we must harness, when we are pushed, angry, and frustrated and want to scream. These are the moments when we should be most passionate and from which our greatest ideas come. Surely we can be better tomorrow than we are today?

I am a big believer in getting comfortable being uncomfortable and consistently putting yourself in situations that will push you to the edge. On that edge, where the pain is so great or the problem causes so much hurt, you cannot simply subscribe to the philosophy of ignorance is bliss for another day or another moment.

I talk to and interview hundreds and hundreds of entrepreneurs, and for the most part, their greatest idea came because they were trying to solve a problem, consumer or otherwise. You've heard the stories before: there were no decent undies for men, so we made our own; my baby hated all of the puréed food in the supermarkets, so we began manufacturing our own recipes; we moved and there wasn't a good café around our new place, so we resigned from our day jobs and opened one.

And it can be similar for problems of a social nature, like the incredible organization Aussie Helpers. It started because a farmer who lost his own farm from a combination of drought in outback Australia and depression knew others were battling the same issues he once was and would need a cup of tea on rough days and a mate making sure they don't make an ill-thought-out decision when the financial pressure gets all too much.

Then there's the A21 Campaign, an organization fighting human trafficking by prosecuting offenders, housing past victims, and educating everyone else about the fact that the average age of a trafficked girl is twelve to fourteen.

It started in an airport terminal in Thessaloniki, Greece, when its founder, Christine Caine, who travels the world almost nonstop as a speaker, saw countless handmade signs for missing people, mostly young girls, as she collected her baggage that day. Perplexed as to why, she dismissed human trafficking as the cause because "that doesn't happen, that's ridiculous." Then she went online and did some research: it is estimated that there are more slaves in the world today (30 million) than ever before.

We must keep questioning ourselves every single day. Why do I do what I do? Why do I want to make money? Why do I appear in the media? Why do I build a profile?

Could it be that our egos are out of control with a perpetual need for external validation? To an extent we all have a need to belong, to feel good enough, to be worthy, to be loved, to be seen. But there is a difference between doing this and not realizing it and doing it while being present, conscious, and acutely aware of the impact you can have as a result.

In my early twenties, I wrote in my journal, "We cannot make positive change by being wallflowers." I think in that moment, my fate was sealed. And I believe the potential to do good far outweighs the few naysayers who may try to bring us down.

Key to this is continuously putting ourselves in situations that challenge and inspire us. At a conference in Amsterdam in 2011, I met the former secretary-general of the United Nations Kofi Annan, and the winner of the Nobel Peace Prize for pioneering modern-day microfinance, Muhammad Yunus.

At that particular conference, WikiLeaks founder Julian Assange also Skyped in from house arrest. To be in the room and in the presence of such game changers and thought leaders of our time was beyond inspiring and reminded me of the importance of purposefully putting ourselves in situations that shake up our realities and mess with our heads (and hearts). It's perhaps no coincidence that it was at this conference that the true seeds of the *Collective Hub*™ were sown.

I recently heard something that resonated with me and it went along the lines of "We can't help the poor by staying poor. We can't help the sick by being sick. We can't help the unhappy by being unhappy, and really, we can't help the world by being small."

Making money gives us freedom and choice, and having a profile gives us a platform from which we have the opportunity and the strength to be able to really make lasting change in this world.

It's bigger than money for money's sake and profile for ego's sake. Surely we are gearing up for something much bigger? Surely we must stay open, be aware, be informed, and consciously look for opportunities to truly make a difference?

Someone recently said to me, "Just work in your grace zone, meaning doing just what you have been purposed to do. Everyone has his own special job to do. Just do that! No need to do anyone else's job. That takes away the opportunity for them to do it. What is in your hand right now that you could use to manifest what is in your heart?"

Some people will need to take a lead, like Brian Egan from Aussie Helpers or Christine from the A21 Campaign. But we must all agree to do the bit that is presented to us, sometimes big, sometimes small.

As a company—and as an individual—I hope that my team will follow this philosophy. That whenever a charity asks us for copies of the magazine or books for events, functions, goody bags, and the like, our answer will always be yes. That I'll always make myself available to speak at charitable events, and that we'll keep preparing and serving meals for those who are staying at the Ronald McDonald House; it is beautifully humbling to cook for parents whose children are clinging to their very fabric of life.

I hope I never stop doing the talks to those suffering from alcohol and drug addiction (reminding them that the hard work is truly worth it—and that I know from personal experience), or the treks to the Western Ghats in India to raise awareness of microfinancing (I'll never forget the clever, tenacious women who had turned Coca-Cola bottles into handbags), or the visits to orphanages (they needed towels—that's all they asked for; we went out and bought them 200).

And I hope that collectively, we will stick to our editorial mandate in the magazine to continually champion the incredible and inspiring work of individuals and organizations in this arena.

For those in business, may we make money so that we can make a difference with it, whether we're the next Bill and Melinda Gates, the next Michael Bloomberg, or the founders of the next Movember or the next Charity: Water. May we consider purpose before profit. May we be the game changers and the thought leaders. May we be the very best of the human spirit we can be.

THINK BIG
& BEYOND
Yourself
MAKE a
DIFFERENCE

GIVE BACK Kindness is KING STAY ON TRACK

NOW GO . . .

Now go,
the
world
is
yours.

Live your life with purpose and passion

Push the limits

Push yourself

Have dreams

Then make them happen

Don't be afraid to fail

Just get up each time you fall

For there is a life out there for you to live

That requires bravery and courage

Someone who's willing to get off their ass and make it happen

Someone who won't let ANYTHING get in their way

Someone who is ready for the challenge and hungry for success.

Now is the time to be daring.
to be disruptive.

ACKNOWLEDGMENTS

A massive heartfelt thank-you to all the people who have loved and supported me through my journey.

A huge thanks goes out to my core team—specifically Claire, Mel, Jade (who all started with me at quite young ages and have grown with me and the business for years and years; without them I could not do what I do every single day), Aimee, Jodie, Kate, and Lila and every member of "Team Collective Hub"—you are like family to me and I'm grateful that we are on this journey together.

Thanks to our extended team of thirty or so distributors and roughly seventy writers around the globe. A special mention goes out to Jodie Frazer, Shayne McNally, Trevor West, Eras Lazanas, Eugenio Paletto, Janet Judge, Dennis Jones, Victoria Harper, Hunter Drinan, and Warren Broom.

Thanks to my incredible family of Mum, Dennis, Dad, Margot, Kate, and Gracie.

Thanks to my besties Donna, Scottie, Jules, Josh, Robbie, Dan, Luke, Aims, Paul, Stephie, David, Maurice, and Gags.

And of course, a huge thank-you to our loyal and amazing readers, who cheer us on and inspire me every single day. Because of all of you, the movement is growing.

ABOUT THE AUTHOR

Lisa Messenger is the vibrant, game-changing CEO and creative director of The Messenger Group, as well as the founder and editor in chief of the *Collective Hub*™ magazine—an entrepreneurial lifestyle magazine distributed in over thirty-seven countries with a mandate to disrupt, challenge, and inspire. She is an established keynote speaker, panelist, and commentator on business and entrepreneurialism; has authored and coauthored over a dozen books; and has worked globally in events, sponsorship, marketing, PR, and publishing. The Messenger Group itself has custom-published more than four hundred books for companies and individuals.

Lisa has trekked across India raising money for charity, ridden camels in the Sahara for fun, and laughed her way through communal showers in the Costa Rican jungle in the name of personal development.

Her passion is to challenge individuals and corporations to change the way they think, take them out of their comfort zone, and prove that there is more than one way to do anything. She encourages entrepreneurial spirit, creativity, and innovation and lives life to the absolute max. Most mornings she wakes up and pinches herself as to how incredible her life is, but Lisa is also acutely aware and honest about the bumps and tumbles along the way. In between being a serial entrepreneur, speaker, and avid traveler, she spends most of her time in Sydney with her beautiful dog, Benny.

LISA AS A SPEAKER

Lisa is fast becoming a leading speaker in the entrepreneurial space.

Her key message is that "anything is possible." Her presentations are highly engaging, active, motivational and get people wanting to jump out of their seats and taking on the world!

Lisa uses tools, anecdotes, stories, how-to's, and humor to take people on the journey.

Some of her speaking topics include:

- Cultivating a killer self-belief
- Finding passion and purpose
- Creating an amazing team culture
- Failing fast
- Strategic partnerships
- Thinking big and going global
- Challenging your personal limits and overall thinking
- Building a personal brand or business
- Disrupting in small business and within a corporation
- Developing a sixth sense
- Investing in yourself

To book Lisa for a speaking engagement or talk with her events team, contact the North Star Way Speakers Bureau at 1-212-698-8888 or visit www.thenorthwaystar.com.

ABOUT *COLLECTIVE HUB*™

Collective Hub™ launched in 2013 as a print magazine, but quickly became a global sensation that is now sold in thirty-seven countries.

A few years on, we have evolved into a true multimedia brand that also encompasses engaging digital platforms, one-of-a-kind events, strategic collaborations, and unique product extensions.

Across it all, our unwavering vision is to uplift and empower our community to live their fullest lives.

We combine style and substance with a fresh perspective on the issues that matter—across business, design, technology, social change, fashion, travel, food, film, and art.

Whether you are looking for a creativity boost, professional advice from industry experts, the most exciting places to experience, or a warm and practical pep talk, we believe *Collective Hub*™ can be your ultimate guide to making an impact in the world.

COLLECTIVEHUB.COM

@lisamessenger #lisamessenger

@collectivehub #collectivehub